Architecture

15-
JY

ARCHITECTURE AS SPACE

by BRUNO ZEVI

ARCHITECTURE

TRANSLATED BY MILTON GENDEL

AS SPACE

HOW TO LOOK AT ARCHITECTURE

EDITED BY JOSEPH A. BARRY

HORIZON PRESS   NEW YORK

TO ALL MY FRIENDS
IN THE MOVEMENT FOR
ORGANIC ARCHITECTURE

CONTENTS

LIST OF PHOTOGRAPHS

7

8

LIST OF DRAWINGS AND PLANS

ARCHITECTURE—THE UNKNOWN

IT IS virtually standard procedure for a history or criticism of architecture to begin with an attack on the layman. Nineteen out of twenty of the books cited in our bibliography open with complaints and apologies, such as:

"The public is interested in painting and music, in sculpture and literature, but not in architecture. The intellectual, who would feel ashamed not to recognize a painter of the rank of Sebastiano del Piombo and who would turn pale at being charged with ignorance of a painting by Matisse or of a poem by Éluard, feels perfectly at ease in confessing that he doesn't know who Buontalenti or Neutra might be"; or

"Newspapers devote whole columns to a new book by Koestler or to an exhibition of Morandi, but ignore the construction of a new building, even if it's the work of a famous architect. Whereas every self-respecting newspaper has regular coverage of music, theater, movies and, at the very least, a weekly art column, architecture remains the great unknown"; or

"Just as no adequate means exist for information about good architecture, so there are no effective means for impeding the construction of architectural horrors. There is a certain censorship for films and for books, but not for the prevention of architectural and urban outrages, which have far more serious and lasting consequences than the publication of a pornographic novel," or, finally,

"Nevertheless [and this is where the apologies come in] while everyone is free to shut off the radio, to walk out on concerts, to shun the movies and the theater, and to stop reading a book, no one can close his eyes to the buildings which form the setting of city life and which set man's stamp on the countryside."

The lack of public interest in architecture cannot be considered inevitable and inherent in human nature[1] or in the nature of a building,[2] so that we need only limit ourselves to the mere statement of such indifference. Undoubtedly there are material difficulties to overcome; and there is an incapacity on the part of architects, historians of architecture and art critics to make themselves apostles of architecture, to spread the love of architecture, if not to the general public, then at least to the cultivated.

Above all there is the physical impossibility of transporting buildings, as one does paintings, to a given place in order to exhibit them. To look at architecture with any system and intelligence one must already have a lively interest in the subject and be provided with a good deal of good will. The average man who visits an historical city and feels duty-bound to admire its buildings makes the rounds according to purely practical considerations: today, in a given quarter, he visits a Baroque church, then a Roman ruin, then a modern square, then an Early Christian basilica; tomorrow he goes to another section of the city and, on the "second day of the tour," as his Baedeker puts it, he falls into the same confusion of distant and different types of unrelated architecture.[3] How many tourists decide to visit all the Byzantine churches today, the Renaissance monuments tomorrow and modern works the day after tomorrow? How many of us can resist the temptation to break the order of our viewing to admire the Romanesque tower that rises behind a Baroque church or to go back into the Pantheon, right there within easy reach of the Gothic pile of Santa Maria sopra Minerva? It is possible to gather from all over the western world the paintings of Titian or of Brueghel and so reveal their special quality in single great exhibitions; it is possible to perform the works of Bach or of Mozart in concerts devoted to them, but an exhibition of Francesco di Giorgio or of Neumann can be put together only at the expense of one's own fatigue, which presupposes a real passion for architecture.

This passion, alas, rarely exists. The tenacity and devotion of archeologists, splendidly praiseworthy in the field of philology, rarely rise to that level of evocative recreation which arouses a sympathetic echo in the public. Professional architects, who, in order to explore the problems of contemporary architecture, must necessarily have a profound

16

passion for architecture in the living sense of the word, are largely lacking today in the specific cultural background which would qualify them for a knowledgeable entry into the arena of historical and critical debate. The culture of modern architects is too often limited by their chronic controversies. In their fight against feebly imitative or falsifying academicism they have more than once, if only unconsciously, declared their lack of interest in the valid works of the past, and in this way have failed to draw from these works the vital, permanent guiding principle without which no avant-garde position might broaden into a whole cultural complex. We are speaking not only of Frank Lloyd Wright and his disparagement of the Italian Renaissance (anything can be forgiven a genius, particularly critical unobjectivity), but also of the cultural inclination of Le Corbusier, whose superficial skimming and impressionistic judgment of various periods in the history of architecture [4] is more an elegant, brilliant intellectual exercise than a fruitful contribution to a critical reevaluation of architecture. *Les yeux qui ne voient pas,* the eyes which do not see the beauty of Purist forms are eyes that today do not see and do not understand the lessons of traditional architecture.

Much remains to be done. It is the task of the second generation of modern architects, once having overcome the psychological break involved in the birth of the functionalist movement, to reestablish a cultural order. The moment of ostentatious novelty and avant-garde manifestos has passed and modern architecture must now take its place in architectural tradition, aiming above all at a critical revision of this very tradition. It has become evident that an organic culture cannot, in dealing with the past and specifically with architectural history, use two standards of judgment, one for modern and another for traditional architecture, if it is, as it must be, designed to provide modern disoriented and rootless man with a base and a history, to integrate individual and social needs which manifest themselves today as an antithesis between freedom and planning, theory and practice. Once we are able to apply the same criteria in evaluating contemporary architecture and that of previous centuries, we shall be taking a decisive step forward in this direction.

With this in mind, it is remarkably enlightening to subject the many books on esthetics, art criticism and the history of architecture to this simple test: to the volumes of an historical character, add a chapter on modern architecture, and see whether the fundamental critical concepts are still valid; to the volumes strongly pro-modern, add chapters on the architecture of the past, and then note the absurdities to which the extension of the purely functionalist or rationalist point of view in criticism would lead.

Few volumes would survive a test of this sort. In fact, most historical works can be eliminated, from the start, for lack of vitality, for inability to address the lively interests of living men without which the history and criticism of architecture become archeology in the dead sense of the word. Many recent books fail this test because of their partiality for the modern or because of the perennially childlike and monotonously ingenuous enthusiasm of those—and there is one born every day—who are still discovering the functionalist revelation. This revelation, now a quarter of a century old, almost generally accepted and culturally absorbed, has finally reached the age of maturity at which time every human being, and every human message, should set itself vaster aims than self-defense.

These, in brief, are the positions of the public, the archeologists and the architects. Now how far along have the art critics come? Apparently they have advanced somewhat. Fifteen years ago, when sociologists and thinkers on the level of Lewis Mumford were already concerning themselves with the problems of historical and contemporary architecture, one rarely found art critics devoting themselves specifically to these problems. Today things are different. We find art critics everywhere who deal almost exclusively with architecture, and a number who are concerned with it periodically. It is significant that architecture is now commonly treated in art magazines, that monthly publications like *Art News* of New York and *The Studio* of London publish a regular review of the most important architectural works, and that there are now architectural experts on the staffs of dailies like the *London Times* and the *New York Times*. In Italy, too, some of the best art critics, men like Argan and Ragghianti, perfectly understand the importance of architecture and are working together to make it more widely known.

But if we probe further into this new development, which at first seems so comforting, we find that beneath the appearance of quantity the substance is often unsatisfactory. And the fundamental reason is the same insufficiency which renders inadequate the chapters on architecture in most histories of art written by art critics.

What is this characteristic defect? It has been said repeatedly: It consists in the fact that buildings are judged as if they were sculpture and painting, that is to say, externally and superficially, as purely plastic phenomena. It is not merely an error of critical method; it is a misconception arising from the lack of a philosophical position. By affirming the unity of the arts and thereby granting to those qualified in one branch of artistic activity the same qualification to understand and to judge *all* works of art, critics extend the methods of evaluating painting to the entire field of the plastic arts and so reduce everything to pictorial values. In this way they fail to consider what is peculiar to architecture and therefore different from sculpture and painting. In other words, they miss the qualities which are uniquely essential to architecture.[5]

In the last half century, particularly in the last thirty years, the renewal of painting which began with Cubism has represented a simplification of the pictorial formula. The movements which followed first proclaimed a liberation from subject and verisimilitude, then heralded the advent of abstract art. That content did not matter was shouted from the housetops, and finally content was eliminated. Line, color, form, volume, mass, space-time, the totem words of modern art criticism, have become popular if vague conversational clichés. It is said that the artist "stylizes" humanity and that the value of modern painting is of an "architectonic" character. This adjective reverberates everywhere with the force of a superficially definitive statement. From a sketch by Van Gogh to a bas-relief by Manzu, from the *Adam* of Epstein to the *Guernica* of Picasso, everything whose expressive form is ordered through synthesis and shows a trend toward simplification of representation, and everything which sets out to render in visual form the essence of some aspect of reality without the addition of adjectives and decoration has been defined as "architectonic." Architecture has in this way come back into fashion, not for its intrinsic qualities, but because "architectonicity" supposedly characterizes recent movements in painting.

The phenomenon will seem less surprising if we consider that, in spite of all esthetic declarations, art criticism has been based largely on representational content. Architecture, on the other hand, has remained uncongenial to the average art critic, because it did not permit him those romantico-psychological evocations in which he could indulge when writing of painting and sculpture; in other words, because he found architecture an "abstract" art. Once modern painting required a reform in its vocabulary of criticism, it was natural to turn precisely to architecture and to music, which, by a superficial and overworked classification, was paired with architecture because of a supposed brotherhood in abstraction.

For those in pursuit of criticism for effect and salon brilliance, this modern confusion of tongues opened infinite possibilities. Even scholars as serious as Giedion took pleasure in comparing the equilibrium of a *danseuse* by Degas with the immobility of the foot of the arches in the Galerie des Machines at the Paris Exposition of 1889, or in coupling a Mondrian painting with a planimetric rendering by Mies van der Rohe, or a curvilinear town plan of Le Corbusier with the volutes of a Borromini or of a Jones. All games of chance, pleasant as intellectual gymnastics, they are little more than play.

No one can stop anyone from talking about the Cubism of Le Corbusier, the Constructivism of the early Terragni, the Neo-Plasticism of Mies. And we may occasionally study such remarks for what they reveal of a vague current in current taste. (Besides, they are almost always entertaining and stimulating.) However, two facts must be recognized: 1) this method continues to apply to architecture criteria used in the criticism of painting, with the sole small difference that the concepts valid for contemporary painting are now applied to contemporary architecture, whereas previously the concepts of traditional painting were applied to traditional architecture; 2) the history and criti-

20

cism of architecture will not advance one step by following this road.

The public ignorance of architecture! The public lack of interest in architecture! How, in the face of such confusion among critics, can we honestly blame the public? Isn't it perhaps the lack of a valid and clear interpretation of architecture that determines public ignorance and lack of interest? If engineers continue to write histories of architecture which are concerned entirely with the history of technical construction, how can we expect the great public to follow them? If archeologists persist in their philological erudition, how can we expect to engage the passions of non-specialists? If, on the other hand, art critics treat architecture as a reflection, an echo of tendencies in painting, why should the public bother with architecture instead of turning directly to the primary sources—painting and sculpture?

If we really want to teach people *how to look at architecture*, we must first of all establish a clarity of method. The average reader, leafing through books on the esthetics and criticism of architecture, is horrified by the vagueness of their terms: *truth, movement, force, vitality, sense of outline, harmony, grace, breadth, scale, balance, proportion, light and shade, eurhythmics, solids and voids, symmetry, rhythm, mass, volume, emphasis, character, contrast, personality, analogy.* These are attributes of architecture which various authors use as classifications without specifying what they refer to. They certainly have a legitimate place in the history of architecture, but on one condition: that the *essence* of architecture be made clear.

This need for a new critical formulation—it need hardly be stated—does not find its first expression in these pages. Apart from the intuitions of the older critics and historians from Lao Tse to Vischer, from Vasari to Goethe, from Schopenhauer to Milizia and Wölfflin, it can be said that every book of architectural criticism contains at least one passage which touches on this need. In the critical literature of recent years these references have become increasingly frequent. Some books, notably those by Pevsner, have opened the way. The present contribution, therefore, does not constitute a discovery. It is intended simply to sum up and clarify recent critical conclusions, to harvest what preceding scholars have sowed with intelligence, patience and labor.

21

II SPACE—PROTAGONIST OF ARCHITECTURE

A SATISFACTORY history of architecture has not yet been written, because we are still not accustomed to thinking in terms of *space*, and because historians of architecture have failed to apply a coherent method of studying buildings from a spatial point of view.

Everyone who has thought even casually about the subject knows that the specific property of architecture—the feature distinguishing it from all other forms of art—consists in its working with a three-dimensional vocabulary which includes man. Painting functions in two dimensions, even if it can suggest three or four. Sculpture works in three dimensions, but man remains apart, looking on from the outside. Architecture, however, is like a great hollowed-out sculpture which man enters and apprehends by moving about within it.

When you want a house built, the architect shows you a rendering of one of the exterior views and perhaps a perspective sketch of the living room. Then he submits plans, elevations and cross-sections; in other words, he represents the architectural volume by breaking it down into the vertical and horizontal planes which enclose and divide it: floors, roof, exterior and interior walls. Our illiteracy regarding space derives mainly from the use of these means of representation, which have been carried over into technical books on the history of architecture and into popular histories of art, where they are supplemented by photographs.

The plan of a building, being nothing more than an abstract projection on a horizontal plane of all its walls, has reality only on paper and is justified only by the necessity of measuring the distances between the various elements of the construction for the practical execution of the work. The façades and cross-sections of the exteriors and interiors serve to measure height. Architecture, however, does not consist in the sum of the width, length and height of the structural elements which enclose space, but in the void itself, the enclosed space in which man lives and moves. What we are doing, then, is to consider as a complete representation of architecture what is nothing more than a practical device used by the architect to put on paper specific measurements for the use of the builder. For the purpose of learning how to look at architecture, this would be more or less equivalent to a method which described a painting by giving the dimensions of its frame, calculating the areas covered by the various colors and then reproducing each color separately.

It is equally obvious that a poem is something more than just a sum of fine verses. To judge a poem, you must study it as a whole, and even if you then proceed to the analysis of each of its verses, you must do it with reference to the context. Anyone entering on the study of architecture must understand that even though a plan may have abstract beauty on paper, the four façades may seem well-balanced and the total volume well-proportioned, the building itself may turn out to be poor architecture. Internal space, that space which, as we shall see in the next chapter, cannot be completely represented in any form, which can be grasped and felt only through direct experience, is the protagonist of architecture. To grasp space, to know how to *see* it, is the key to the understanding of building. Until we have learned not only to understand space theoretically, but also to apply this understanding as a central factor in the criticism of architecture, our history, and thus our enjoyment, of architecture will remain haphazard. We shall continue to flounder in a critical language which describes buildings in terms proper only to painting and sculpture.[6] At best we shall be praising space as abstractly imagined and not as concretely experienced.[7] Studies and research will be limited to philological contributions, such as the study of social factors (function), constructional data (technics), volumetric or decorative characteristics (plastic and pictorial elements). These contributions are unquestionably highly useful, but they are ineffectual in communicating the value of architecture, if we omit its spatial essence. Our use of words like *rhythm, scale, balance, mass* will continue to be vague until we have succeeded in giving them meaning specific to the reality which defines architecture, and that is: space.

23

An enormous and certainly disproportionate number of pages devoted to architecture in textbooks on art deal with the sculptural, pictorial, social and sometimes even the psychological history (through the study of artists' personalities) of buildings; not with their architectural reality or with their spatial essence. Of course, such material has its value. For example, anyone unacquainted with Italian who wishes to read the *Divine Comedy* will, obviously, find it useful to learn the meaning of its words and, by studying the syntax of Medieval Italian, learn the meaning of its sentences. It would be useful, as well, to learn the history and theology of the Middle Ages, the material and psychological vicissitudes in the life of Dante. But it would be absurd to forget, in the course of these preparatory labors, one's original motivation and final purpose, which is to relive the *Divine Comedy*. All archeological and philological study is useful only insofar as it prepares and enriches the ground for an integrated history of architecture.[8]

What, then, is architecture? And, perhaps equally important, what is non-architecture? Is it proper to identify architecture with a beautiful building and non-architecture with an ugly building? Is the distinction between architecture and non-architecture based on purely esthetic criteria? And what is "space," which we are calling "the protagonist of architecture"? How many dimensions does it have?

These are the basic questions which present themselves in formulating a criticism of architecture. We shall try to answer them by beginning with the last, which is the most specific.

The façade and walls of a house, church or palace, no matter how beautiful they may be, are only the container, the box formed by the walls; *the content is the internal space*. In America, schools of industrial design teach the art and craft of designing packages, but none of them has ever thought of confusing the value of the box with the value of what it contains. In many cases, container and contained are mutually interdependent, as in a French Gothic cathedral or in the majority of genuinely modern buildings, but this cannot be taken as a rule, because it is not true of a vast number of buildings, notably those of the Baroque period. Frequently in the course of the history of architecture, we find buildings which show a clear discrepancy between container and contained, and even a hasty analysis will show that often, in fact too often, the box formed by the walls has been the object of more thought and labor than the architectural space itself.[9] Now, then, how many dimensions does this building-container have? Can they be legitimately identified with the dimensions of the space contained, which is architecture?

The discovery of *perspective* or graphic representation in three dimensions—height, width, depth—led Renaissance artists of the fifteenth century to believe they had finally mastered the dimensions of architecture and the means of reproducing them. The buildings illustrated in *pre*-Renaissance painting do, in fact, look flat and distorted. Giotto took great pains to put architectural backgrounds into his frescoes, but technically his success was only relative. (He knew, of course, how to turn his limitation to good esthetic account, emphasizing flat chromatic design which would have been completely altered had he known and used three-dimensional representation.) At that time painters still worked in two dimensions, but the rigid frontality of the Byzantine was giving way to a more naturalistic style, at least in the figures. A greater ability to paint pictorial passages from light to dark made it possible to transfer to a flat surface the results of plastic experiments in sculpture. In Pisan architecture the surfaces of cathedral façades were broken and given depth, as well as chromatic vibrancy, through the use of superimposed rows of colonnettes. Not before the discovery of perspective, however, was it possible to achieve an adequate representation of architectural interiors or exteriors. Once the laws of perspective had been elaborated, the problem appeared to be solved: architecture, it was said, has three dimensions; here is the method of drawing them, which anyone can use. From the time of Masaccio, Fra Angelico and Benozzo Gozzoli to Bramante and the Baroque masters on up to the nineteenth century, innumerable painters worked along with designers and architects to represent architecture in perspective.

When, in the last decade of the nineteenth century, the reproduction of photographs, and thus their mass distribution, became a simple process, photographers took the place of draftsmen, and a click of the shutter replaced those perspectives which enthusiastic students of architecture had been laboriously tracing ever since the Renaissance. But at that very moment, when everything seemed critically clear and technically perfect, the mind of man discovered that a *fourth* dimension existed in addition to the three dimensions of perspective. This was the Cubist revolution in the concept of space, which took place shortly before the first World War.

We shall not take more time in discussing the fourth dimension than is strictly necessary for our purpose. The Paris painter of the late 1900's reasoned more or less as follows: "I see and represent an object, for example a box or a table. I see it from one point of view. But if I hold the box in my hands and turn it, or if I walk around the table, my point of view changes, and to represent the object from each new viewpoint I must draw a new perspective of it. The reality of the object, therefore, is not exhausted by its representation in the three dimensions of one perspective. To capture it completely, I must draw an infinite number of perspectives from the infinite points of view possible." This successive displacement *in time* of the angle of vision adds a new dimension to the three dimensions of tradition. Thus *time* was baptized the "fourth dimension." (The means used by Cubist painters to render the fourth dimension—superimposing the images of an object seen from various points of view, in order to project them all simultaneously on canvas—do not concern us here.)

The Cubists were not content with the plural representation of the exterior of an object. Their passion for discovery, for grasping the total reality of an object, led them to the following thought: in every physical structure there is not only an external form, there is also an internal organism; besides the skin, there are the muscles and the skeleton, the internal constitution. And so in their paintings they show simultaneously not only the external aspects of a box, for example, but also the box in plan, the box exploded, the box smashed.

The Cubist conquest of the fourth dimension is of immense historical importance quite apart from the esthetic evaluation that can be made for or against Cubist painting. You may prefer a Byzantine mosaic to a fresco of Mantegna without thereby denying the importance of perspective in the development of experiments in dimension. Similarly,

26

it is possible to dislike the paintings of Picasso and still recognize the value of the fourth dimension. The fourth dimension has had a decided application to architecture, not so much for the translation of the pictorial language of the Cubists into architectural terms in the early stages of the modern French and German movements, as for the scientific support it has given to the critical distinction between real buildings and buildings on paper, between architecture and stage designing—a distinction which for a long time had been problematical.

The concept of the fourth dimension seemed to end, once and for all, the search for dimensions characteristic of architecture. To examine a statuette, we pick it up and turn it in our hands. We look at it from all angles. We walk around larger figures and groups to examine them from all sides, close-up and from a distance. In architecture, it was reasoned, there is the same element of time. In fact, this element is indispensable to architecture: from the first hut to the modern house, from the cave of primitive man to the church, school or office of today, no work of architecture can be experienced and understood without the fourth dimension, without the time needed for our walk of discovery within it. The problem again appeared to be solved.

However, a dimension common to all the arts obviously cannot be peculiar to any one of them, and therefore architectural space cannot be thought of entirely in terms of four dimensions. This new factor of *time* has, in fact, a meaning in architecture which is antithetical to its meaning in painting.

In painting, the fourth dimension is a quality *inherent* in the representation of an object, an element of its reality which a painter may choose to project on a flat surface without requiring physical participation on the part of the observer.

The same thing is true of sculpture: in sculpture the "movement" of a form, for example by Boccioni, is a quality *inherent* in the statue we are looking at, which we must relive visually and psychologically.

But in architecture we are dealing with a concrete phenomenon which is entirely different: here, man *moving about within the building*, studying it from successive points of views, himself creates, so to speak, the fourth dimension, giving the space an integrated reality.[10]

27

Elaborate treatises have of course been written on the subject; our problem here is simply to give a clear explanation of an experience familiar to everyone. To be more precise, the fourth dimension is sufficient to define the architectural volume, that is, the box formed by the walls which enclose space. But the space itself—the essence of architecture—transcends the limits of the four dimensions.

How many dimensions, then, does space, this architectural "void," have? Five, ten, an infinite number perhaps. For our purpose it is enough to establish that architectural space cannot be defined in terms of the dimensions of painting and sculpture. The phenomenon of space becomes concrete reality only in architecture and therefore constitutes its specific character.

Having arrived at this point, the reader will understand that the question, "What is architecture?", has already been answered. To say, as is usual, that architecture is "beautiful building" and that non-architecture is "ugly building" does not explain anything, because "ugly" and "beautiful" are relative terms. It would be necessary, in any case, first to formulate an analytic definition of "What is a building?", which would mean starting once more from the beginning.

The most exact definition of architecture that can be given today is that which takes into account *interior space*. Beautiful architecture would then be architecture in which the interior space attracts us, elevates us and dominates us spiritually (as in the case of Chartres Cathedral); ugly architecture would be that in which the interior space disgusts and repels us (you might prefer to choose your own example). But the important thing is to establish that no work lacking interior space can be considered architecture.

If we admit this much—and to admit it seems to be a matter of common sense, not to say of logic—we must recognize that most histories of architecture are full of observations that have nothing to do with architecture in this specific meaning. They devote page after page to the façades of buildings which in effect are sculpture on a large scale, but have little to do with architecture in the *spatial* sense of the word. An obelisk, a fountain, a monument, a bridge, big as they may be—a portal, a triumphal arch—are all works of art which are discussed in histories of architecture although they are not properly architecture. Architectural backdrops or any sort of painted or drawn architecture are not true architecture any more than a play not yet put into dialogue, but only sketched in its broad outlines, can be regarded as a dramatic performance. In other words, the experience of space is not communicated until the actual mechanical expression has rendered material the poetic conception. Were we to take any history of architecture and severely prune it of everything not strictly concerned with architecture, it is certain that we should have to do away with at least eighty out of every hundred pages.

At this point, two serious misunderstandings may arise in the mind of the reader which would not only destroy the value of the preceding argument, but would even make the interpretation of architecture as space ridiculous. They are:

1) that architectural space can be experienced only in the interior of a building, and therefore urban or city-planned space, for all practical purposes, does not exist or have any value;

2) that space is not only the protagonist of architecture, but represents the *whole* of architectural experience, and that consequently the interpretation of a building in terms of space is the *only* critical tool required in judging architecture.

These two possible misunderstandings must be cleared up immediately:

The experience of space, which we have indicated as characteristic of architecture, has its extension in the city, in the streets, squares, alleys and parks, in the playgrounds and in the gardens, wherever man has defined or limited a *void* and so has created an enclosed space. If, in the interior of a building, space is defined by six planes (floor, ceiling and four walls), this does not mean that a void enclosed by five planes instead of six—as, for example, a (roofless) courtyard or public square—cannot be regarded with equal validity as space. It is doubtful whether the experience of space one has in riding in an automobile along a straight highway through miles of uninhabited flatland can be defined as an architectural experience in our present use of the term, but it is certain that all urban space wherever the view is screened off, whether by stone walls or rows of trees or embankments, presents the same features we find in architectural space.

Since every architectural volume, every structure of walls, constitutes a boundary, a pause in the continuity of space, it is clear that every building functions in the creation of two kinds of space: its internal space, completely defined by the building itself, and its external or urban space, defined by that building and the others around it. It is evident then that all those subjects which we have excluded as not being true architecture—bridges, obelisks, fountains, triumphal arches, groups of trees and, in particular, the façades of buildings—are brought into play in the creation of urban space. The specific esthetic value of these elements must remain a question of minor importance until we clear up our second misunderstanding. What interests us at the present point in our discussion is their function in determining an enclosed space. Just as four beautifully decorated walls do not in themselves create a beautiful environment, so a group of excellent houses can define a poor urban space, and *vice versa.*[11]

The second possible misunderstanding would carry our argument to a *reductio ad absurdum* with conclusions totally foreign to our intention in proposing a spatial interpretation of architecture. To maintain that internal space is the essence of architecture does not mean that the value of an architectural work rests *entirely* on its spatial values. Every building can be characterized by a plurality of values: economic, social, technical, functional, esthetic, spatial and decorative. Anyone is free to write economic, social, technical or volumetric histories of architecture, in the same way that it is possible to write a cosmological, Thomistic or political analysis of the *Divine Comedy*.

The reality of a work of art, however, is in the *sum* of all these factors; and a valid history cannot omit any of them. Even if we neglect the economic, social and technical factors, it is clear that space in itself, although it is the principal element in architecture, is not enough to define it. While it is incontestable that beautiful decoration will never create beautiful space, it is also true that a satisfactory space, if it is not complemented by an adequate treatment of the walls which enclose it, is not sufficient to create an esthetic environment. It is common to see a beautiful room ruined by badly used colors, unsuitable furniture or poor lighting. Doubtless, these elements are of relatively little importance; they can easily be changed, whereas the space remains fixed. But an esthetic judgment of a building is based both on its specific architectural value and on the various secondary factors, which may be sculptural, as in applied or three-dimensional decoration, pictorial, as in the case of mosaics, frescoes and easel paintings or on other factors, such as furniture.

After a century of predominantly decorative, sculptural and a- or non-spatial architecture, the modern movement, with the splendid intent of returning architecture to the expression proper to it, banished decoration from building, insisting on the thesis that volumetric and spatial values are the only values legitimate to architecture. (European Functionalism emphasized volumetric values in architecture; the Organic Movement was more concerned with those of space.)

If it is clear, then, that as architects we should not underscore the *decorative* rather than the *spatial* in architecture, then as critics and historians we should not advance our preferences or dislikes in the field of decorative or figurative means and expressions as the sole yardstick for our judgment of architecture of all periods. This is all the more true because decoration (not in the form of applied ornamentation, but in the new play of contrasting natural materials, in the new sense of color, and so on) is now, quite properly, coming back into architecture after twenty years of architectural nudism, glacial volumetrics, stylistic sterilization and the purging of decorative details, contrary to psychological and spiritual needs. "Freedom from decoration," as an architectural program, can be no more than a polemical, and therefore ephemeral, slogan.

At this point the uninitiated reader will, perhaps, feel confused. If decoration has some importance, if sculpture and painting, earlier thrown out, reappear in the field of architecture, what end has our discussion served? It has not been to invent esoteric theories about architecture, but simply to put order and system into current ideas intuitively felt by everyone. Certainly decoration, sculpture and painting enter into the study of buildings (no less than economic causes, social or functional values and technical considerations). Everything figures in architecture, as it does in every great human phenomenon of art, thought or practice. But how? Not without differentiation, as one might believe in asserting a generic and vacuous unity of all the arts. Decorating, sculpture and painting enter into the grammar of architecture in their proper places as adjectives, not as substantives.

The history of architecture is primarily the history of spatial conceptions. Judgment of architecture is fundamentally judgment of the internal space of buildings. If, because of its lack of interior space, a work cannot be judged on this basis, as in the case of the types of constructions mentioned above, the structure or building—be it the Arch of Titus, the Column of Trajan or a fountain by Bernini—falls outside the history of architecture and belongs properly, as a volumetric entity, to the history of urbanism; and, with respect to its intrinsic artistic value, to the history of sculpture. If judgment of its internal space proves negative, the structure falls into the category of non-architecture, even if its decorative elements can be treated as belonging to the history of truly fine sculpture. If judgment of its architectural space is positive, the building must be included in the history of architecture, even if the decoration is ineffectual; even if, that is to say, the building as a whole is not entirely satisfactory. When, finally, the judgment of the spatial conception of a building, of its volumetrics and of its decorative quality, proves positive, we are then in the presence of one of those rare, integral works of art in which all the figurative means combine in a superlative artistic creation.

In conclusion, even if the other arts contribute to architecture, it is *interior space*, the space which surrounds and includes us, which is the basis for our judgment of a building, which determines the "yea" or "nay" of esthetic pronouncement on architecture. All the rest is important or perhaps we should say *can* be important, but always in a subordinate relation to the spatial idea. Whenever critics and historians lose sight of this hierarchy, they create confusion and accentuate the present disorientation in architecture.

That space—void—should be the protagonist of architecture is after all natural. Architecture is not art alone, it is not merely a reflection of conceptions of life or a portrait of systems of living. Architecture is environment, the stage on which our lives unfold.

32

G. Sacconi: Monument to Victor Emanuel II, Rome (1885-1911).

Plate 1. Architecture without internal space

Arch of Titus in the Roman Forum, Rome (81 A.D.).

33

E. Gallori: Monument to Garibaldi, Rome
(1895).

Pietro Bernini: Fountain of the "Baraccia" in the Piazza di Spagna, Rome (17th century).

Plate 1. Architecture without internal space

Aqueduct of Claudius (52 A.D.) seen from the Via Appia Nuova, Rome.

Plate 1. Architecture without internal space

36

Column of Marcus Aurelius in the Piazza Colonna, Rome (2nd century A.D.).

Bridge of Castelvecchio, Verona (1354-56).

Plate 1. Architecture without internal space

Pyramid of Caius Cestus, Rome (15 B.C.).

Plate 1. Architecture without internal space

Fountains in the park of the Villa Trissino, near Vicenza (18th century).

A. Sangallo il Giovane and Michelangelo: Palazzo Farnese, Rome (1514-47).

Plate 2. Surface and volume as represented in photographs

Le Corbusier and P. Jean-
neret: Villa, Garches (1927).

40

Plate 2. Surface and volume as represented in photographs

Castle Ursino, Catania (13th century).

Plate 2. Surface and volume as represented in photographs

F. Ll. Wright: Falling Water, Bear Run, Penna. (1936).

Fondaco dei Turchi, Venice (13th century), before restoration.

Plate 2. Surface and volume as represented in photographs

43

Nello Aprile, Cino Calcaprina, Aldo Cardelli,
Mario Fiorentino, Giuseppe Perugini: Monument at the Cave Ardeatine, Rome (1945).

Michelangelo: Piazza del Campidoglio,
Rome (1546-47).

Plate 2. Surface and volume as represented in photographs

THE REPRESENTATION OF SPACE

ONE DAY, sometime in the 1430's, Johann Gutenberg of Mainz conceived the idea of engraving the letters of the alphabet on little pieces of wood and of putting them together to form words, lines, phrases, pages. He invented printing and so opened up to the masses the world of poetry and literature, until then the property and instrument of a restricted class of intellectuals.

In 1839, Daguerre applied his knowledge of photo-chemistry to the problem of reproducing images of an object. He invented photography and marked the passage from the aristocratic to the collective plane of a vast amount of visual experience hitherto available only to the few who could afford to employ an artist to paint their portraits or who could travel to study works of painting and sculpture.

In 1877, Edison invented a cylindrical apparatus and succeeded for the first time in recording sound on a sheet of tin-foil. Forty-three years later, in 1920, the first radio broadcast took place. The art of music, previously at the exclusive command of limited groups of connoisseurs, was by means of the phonograph and the radio made accessible to the great public.

Thus, a continuous scientific and technological progress made possible the large-scale diffusion of poetry and literature, painting, sculpture and music, enriching the spiritual heritage of an ever increasing number of people. Just as the reproduction of sound has by now almost reached perfection, so the progress of color photography indicates that the next few years will show a distinct elevation of general education in chromatic values, a phase of visual experience in which the average level of understanding is still much lower than it is with regard to drawing and composition.

Architecture, however, remains isolated and alone. The problem of how to represent space, far from being solved, has not as yet been even stated. Since up to now there has been no clear conception or definition of the nature and consistency of architectural space, the need for its representation and mass diffusion has consequently not been felt. This is one more reason for the inadequacy of architectural education.

As we have seen, the methods of representing buildings most frequently employed in histories of art and architecture consist of (1) plans, (2) façades and elevations and (3) photographs. We have already stated that neither singly nor together can these means ever provide a complete representation of architectural space. But, in the absence of thoroughly satisfactory methods, it becomes our concern to study the techniques we have at hand and to make them more effective than ever. Let us discuss them in detail and at length:

1) *Plans.* We have said that a plan is an abstraction entirely removed from any real experience of a building. Nevertheless, a plan is still the sole way we have of evaluating the architectural organism as a whole. And every architect knows that the plan, however insufficient in itself, has a distinct primacy in determining the artistic worth of a building. Le Corbusier, speaking of the "plan générateur," does nothing to advance the understanding of architecture; quite the contrary, he is engendering in his followers a sort of mystique of the "esthetic of the plan," scarcely less formalistic than that of the Beaux Arts. However, his concept is based on fact. The plan is still among the basic tools in the representation of architecture. The question is how to go about improving it.

Let us take, for example, Michelangelo's planimetric design for St. Peter's in Rome. Many books reprint Bonanni's plan (fig. 1), partly because of a snobbish vogue for old prints and drawings (a vogue which plays no small part, particularly in the history of city planning, in increasing the general confusion) and partly because the authors of the books do not bother to investigate the problems involved in the representation of architecture. Yet no one after some thought can say that Bonanni's plan is the most satisfactory representation of Michelangelo's spatial conception for the young man who is beginning his study of architecture or for the general reader who is naturally asking the critic and historian to help him understand architectural values.

46

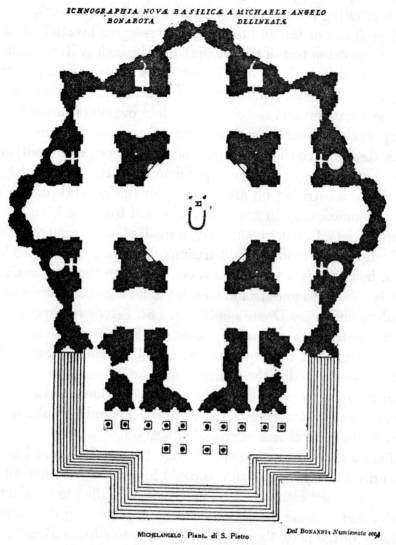

TABVLA 17.

ICHNOGRAPHIA NOVÆ BASILICÆ A MICHAELE ANGELO
BONAROTA   *DELINEATÆ*

MICHELANGELO: Pianta di S. Pietro   *Dal* BONANNI: *Numismata ecc.*

Fig. 1. Michelangelo: Design for St. Peter's, Rome (ca. 1520). Plan (by Bonanni).

To begin with, this plan shows an abundance of details, a minute marking of every pilaster and every curve, all of which may be useful in a later stage of the critical commentary (when it becomes our concern to ascertain whether the spatial theme is given a consistent elaboration in the decoration and plastic treatment of the walls), but which

47

is confusing, at this point, when all our efforts should be directed toward illustrating the spatial basis of the architectural work.

A professor of Italian literature does not give his students a complete, unannotated text of the *Divine Comedy*, saying, "Here is the masterpiece—read and admire it." There is first a long phase of preparatory work—we learn about Dante's subject matter from the summaries in our school texts on literature—we accustom ourselves to the language of the period and poet through selections in anthologies. Literary pedagogues devote a considerable part of their labors to simplifying the material, whereas the analogous problem is for the most part ignored by pedagogues writing on architecture for the general public. To be sure, it is unnecessary to summarize a sonnet from the *Vita Nuova,* or any brief poetic fragment; similarly, a small villa or country house can readily be understood without a simplified plan. Michelangelo's St. Peter's, however, is a work no less complex than the *Divine Comedy,* and it is difficult to understand why it should take three years of study to analyze and enjoy Dante's epic, when St. Peter's is disposed of in a hasty reference in the course of a lesson on High Renaissance architecture. The gross lack of proportion between the time spent on literature and the time devoted to the explanation of architecture has no justification in criticism (it takes longer to understand Borromini's S. Ivo alla Sapienza than Victor Hugo's *Les Misérables*) and has ultimately resulted in our general lack of spatial education.

Before the performance of a tragedy, the Greeks listened to its plot summarized in a prologue and so could follow the dénouement of the play without that element of curiosity which is alien to contemplative serenity and esthetic judgment. Moreover, possessing the theme and substance of the play, they were better able to admire its artistic realization, the value of every detail and modification. In architectural education some method of graphic summary is undeniably necessary, even if limited to the technique of representation offered by the plan. The whole, after all, precedes its dissection, structure comes before finishing touches, space before decoration. To aid the layman in understanding a plan by Michelangelo, the process of criticism must follow the same direction as Michelangelo's own creative process. Figure 2 shows a

48

summarized version of the plan in figure 1 according to one interpretation (any summary implies an interpretation). Although a hundred better versions might be drawn, what matters is that every historian of architecture should consider it his duty to work out this norm of instructive simplification.

We now come to a far more significant matter. The walls, shown in black on the plan, separate the exterior or urbanistic space from the interior or properly architectural space. Every building, in fact, breaks the continuity of space, sharply divides it in such a way that a man on the inside of the box formed by the walls cannot see what is outside, and *vice versa*. Therefore, every building limits the freedom of the observer's view of space. However, the essence of architecture and thus the element which should be underlined in presenting the plan of a building, does not lie in the material limitation placed on spatial freedom, but in the way space is organized into meaningful form through this process of limitation. Figure 2, no less than figure 1, emphasized the structural mass, that is, the limits themselves, the obstructions which determine the perimeter of possible vision, rather than the "void" in which this vision is given play and in which the essential value of Michelangelo's creation is expressed. Since black attracts the eye more readily than white, these two planimetric representations (figures 2 and 3) may appear at first sight to be just the opposite, the photographic negative, so to speak, of an adequate representation of space.

Actually, this is a mistake. If we look at figure 3, we shall see that it is no improvement on figure 2; it is still the walls, the limits, the frame of the picture, not the picture itself, which are brought out. Why? For the simple reason that interior and exterior space are not distinguished from each other in the representation and no account is taken of the absolute and irreconcilable contradiction which exists between the two kinds of space. Being in a position to see the one means being unable to see the other.

By now the reader will have understood where we want to go. In figures 4 and 5 he will find two planimetric representations of Michelangelo's conception. Figure 4 gives the interior space at the spectator's level; it presents the space in terms of a man walking around inside the building. Figure 5, on the other hand, shows the exterior space, which is defined by the outer walls of the basilica, and which, of course, means nothing in itself, since urbanistic space is not shaped around a single building, but is realized in the voids bounded by all elements, natural and constructed—trees, walls, and so forth—that surround them.

Figure 4, particularly in comparison with the characterlessness of figure 1, may strike us as interesting, but gives rise to the objection that in representing the entire *void* as one uniform black spot, it fails to give

Figs. 2 and 3. Simplified version of the plan in fig. 1 and negative.

any idea of the hierarchy of heights within the space. Apart from the fact that it errs in including, though sketched in lightly, the space of the portico, which cannot be experienced simultaneously with that of the church, it does not separate the space determined by the central cupola, which is very high, from the spaces defined by the four small cupolas at the corners, and these, in turn, from the aisles and niches. Figure 4 would be acceptable if the basilica were all of uniform height, but since there are very marked differences in the heights of various parts of the church, and these are of decisive importance in the determination of spatial values, it follows that even in a plan some attempt

50

must be made to project the forms produced by these differences in height. Some books give figure 6, in which the fundamental structures articulating the organism of the church are shown schematically. This projection represents a step in the right direction with respect to figure 1, in spite of the fact that it retains all the defects we have pointed out as contained in figures 2 and 3.

It may also reasonably be objected that stating an antithesis between interior and exterior space, as illustrated in figures 4 and 5, is

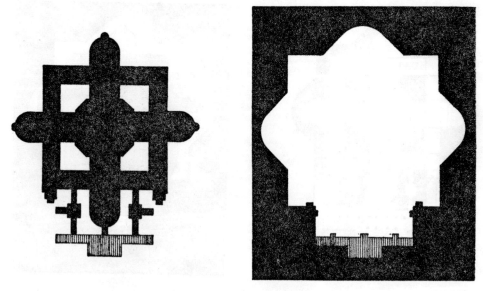

Figs. 4 and 5. The internal and external space of fig. 1.

somewhat arbitrary and polemic. Michelangelo did not first conceive the inside of the basilica, then the outside, separately. He created the whole organism simultaneously and if it is true that seeing the interior space of a building automatically means not seeing its exterior, it is also true that this gap is to a certain extent closed by the "fourth dimension" of time employed in seeing the edifice from successive points of view; the observer does not always remain on the inside or outside of a building, but walks from one to the other. In a building erected during different periods or by different architects, where one has created the interior and another the façades, the distinction and antithesis estab-

51

lished in figures 4 and 5 may be legitimate. But works of unitary conception are marked by a coherence, interdependence and, it might almost be said, an *identity* between interior space and volume; this latter, in turn, is a factor in urbanistic space. The two originate in one inspiration, one theme, one work of art.

With this we come to the heart of the problem of space and its planimetric representation. One author may consider that the most important element to be underlined is the cross-shape of St. Peter's

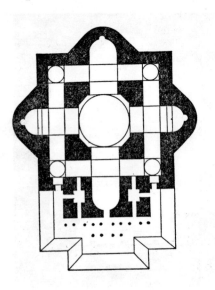 

Figs. 6 and 7. The plan of fig. 1 as a projection of the fundamental structure and as a spatial interpretation.

and will draw a plan like figure 7. Another might see fit to underscore the architectural predominance of the central cupola and the square formed by the aisles, as in the interpretation of figure 8. A third might give greater importance to the four cupolas and the vaults, and will produce a plan such as in figure 9. Each of these interpretations expresses a real element in the space created by Michelangelo, but each is incomplete in itself. However, if our investigation of the problem of representing space is broadened along these lines, there is no doubt that although we may never succeed in discovering a method of fully rendering a conception of space in a plan, we shall nevertheless achieve better results in teaching and learning how to understand space and how to look at architecture by analyzing and discussing the means we have than if we merely neglect the problems they offer and limit ourselves to reproducing figure 1.

2) *Façades.*   The line of reasoning followed in our discussion of *plans* can be repeated in a simpler way when we deal with *elevations.* Here

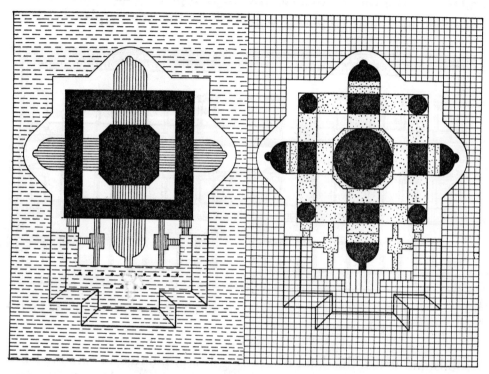

Figs. 8 and 9. Two more spatial interpretations of Michelangelo's plan for St. Peter's.

the basic problem is to represent an object which has two, or at most three, dimensions. Skimming through books on architecture, you will find the graphic linear method very commonly used, as for example in Letarouilly's drawing of the façade of Palazzo Farnese (fig. 10) or in the sketched elevation of Frank Lloyd Wright's Falling Water (fig. 11). It would be difficult to conceive a representational method less thoughtful or less fruitful.

The problem of representing the façade of Palazzo Farnese involves only two dimensions, as we are dealing with a wall surface. Therefore our only concern is how to render the voids and the different textures of the materials employed (plaster, stone, glass) and the degree to which they reflect light. In figure 10 the problem is completely ignored. No distinction is made in representing the various materials. A smooth wall, the space surrounding the building, and the window openings are all shown as if they were alike. Although in present-day discussions of architecture much emphasis is placed on the counterplay between

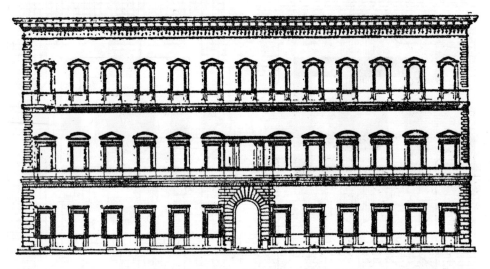

Fig. 10. A. da Sangallo and Michelangelo: Elevation of Palazzo Farnese, Rome (1515–30). Drawing by Letarouilly.

solids and voids, this kind of drawing is still pointed to as a model of clarity. We have rejected the 19th-century pictorial and scenic sketch of a building in the name of greater precision, but on the other hand we have lapsed into an abstract graphic style which is decidedly anti-architectural. In fact, as we are dealing here with a problem clearly sculptural in nature, a representation of this sort is equivalent to rendering a statue by drawing nothing but its outline on paper.

Figure 11 shows a building in which the structure, rather than being confined to a simple stereometric form, is developed with extraordinary organic richness in projections and returns, in planes suspended and intersecting in space. Here we see that the method of

54

representation in figure 11 is hopelessly inadequate to the subject. No layman, not even an architect, highly skilled in visualizing an architectural conception on the basis of its drawings, could ever gather from this design what Falling Water really looks like.

Reproducing the drawing of a façade in its photographic negative is of no more use than it was for us in the case of a plan. Figure 12, the negative of figure 10, has the same shortcomings as its positive. The solution must be something on the order of figure 13, in which the

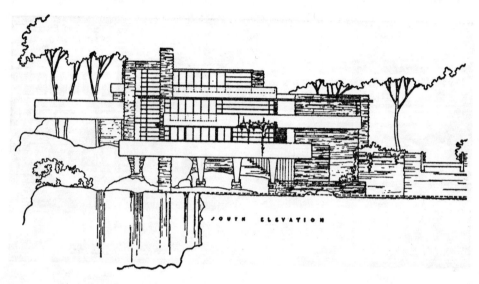

Fig. 11 F. Ll. Wright: Elevation of Falling Water, Bear Run, Penna. (1936).

material entity of the building is detached from the surrounding sky, the relatively transparent voids of the windows are distinguished from the opaque wall surfaces, and the various materials are distinguished from each other.

Nothing can be done, however, greatly to improve figure 11. It would be absurd to try to clarify the representation of Frank Lloyd Wright's volumetric play by adding light and shade. Figure 14, in which this has been done, is little more effective than figure 13. It is clear that this technique of representation is entirely incapable of rendering a complex architectural organism, whether it be the Cathedral of Durham, a church of Neumann or a building of Wright. The method of representation must be substantially different. In each of these cases, the box formed by the walls cannot be divided into simple planes or walls independent of each other, because it is a projection of the internal space; the construction is conceived primarily in terms of volumetrics. We are dealing with plastic volumetric conceptions which can be represented only by models. The evolution of modern sculpture, of Constructivist, Neo-Plastic and to some extent Futurist experiments, and of research in the simultaneity, juxtaposition and

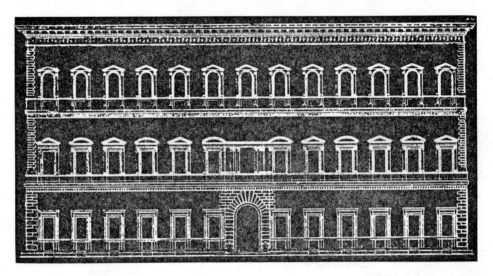

Fig. 12. Negative of fig. 10.

interpenetration of volumes, all provide us with the instruments necessary for this type of representation.

On the other hand, we cannot say that models are completely satisfactory. They are very useful and ought to be used extensively in teaching architecture. However they are inadequate, because they neglect an element crucial to any spatial conception: *the human parameter—* interior and exterior human scale.

For models to be perfect, we should have to suppose that the value of an architectural composition depended entirely on the relations existing between its various components, without reference to the spectator; that, for example, if a palace is beautiful, its elements can be repro-

56

duced exactly in their original proportions, reduced, however, to the scale of a piece of furniture, a beautiful piece of furniture, at that.

This is patently mistaken. The character of any architectural work is determined both in its internal space and in its external volume by the fundamental factor of *scale,* the relation between the dimensions of a building and the dimensions of man. Every building is qualified by its scale. Therefore, not only are three-dimensional models inadequate in representing a building, but any imitation, any transference, of its

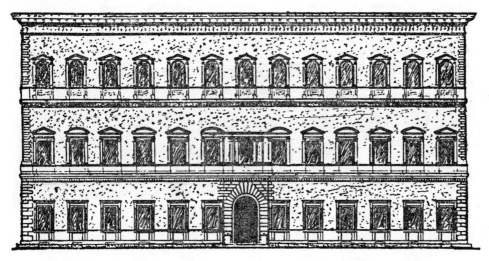

Fig. 13. An interpretation of fig. 10.

decorative and compositional schemes to organically different structures (we have all of 19th-century eclecticism to prove it) turns out to be poor and empty, a sorry parody of the original.

3) *Photographs.*   As photography to a large extent solves the problem of representing on a flat surface the two dimensions of painting and the three dimensions of sculpture, so it faithfully reproduces the great number of two- and three-dimensional elements in architecture, *everything,* that is, *but internal space.* The views, for example, in plate 2 give us an effective idea of the wall surface of Palazzo Farnese and the volumetric values of Falling Water.

But if, as we hope to have made clear by now, the characteristic value of an architectural work consists in our experiencing its internal space from successive points of view, it is evident that no number of photographs can ever constitute a complete pictorial rendition of a building, for the same reason that no number of drawings could do so. A photograph records a building *statically,* as seen from a single standpoint, and excludes the dynamic, almost musical, succession of points of view movingly experienced by the observer as he walks in and around a building. Each photograph is like a single phrase taken out of

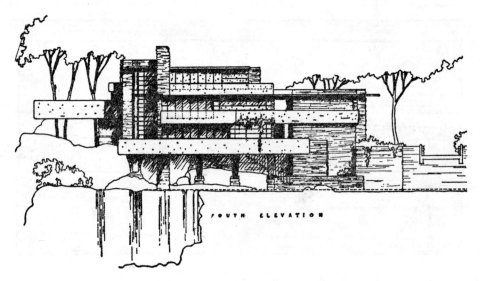

Fig. 14. An interpretation of fig. 11.

the context of a symphony or of a poem, a single frozen gesture of an intricate ballet, where the essential value must be sought in the movement and totality of the work. Whatever the number of still photographs, there is no sense of dynamic motion. (See plates 3 and 4.)

Photographs, of course, have a great advantage over three-dimensional models of conveying some idea of scale, particularly when a human figure is included, but suffer from the disadvantage, even in the case of aerial views, of being unable to give a complete picture of a building.

The researches of Edison and the Lumière brothers in the 1890's led to the invention of a camera geared to carry film forward continuously, so that a series of exposures could be taken in rapid succession, making it possible for photography to render an illusion of motion. This discovery of the motion picture was of enormous importance in the representation of architectonic space, because properly applied it resolves, in a practical way, almost all the problems posed by the fourth dimension. If you go through a building photographing it with a motion picture camera and then project your film, you will be able to recapture, to a large extent, the spatial experience of walking through the building. Motion pictures are consequently taking their proper place in education and it seems likely that in teaching the history of architecture, the use of films, rather than of books, will greatly advance general spatial education.

Plans, façades, cross-sections, models, photographs and films—these are our means of representing space. Once we have grasped the basic nature of architecture, each of these methods may be explored, deepened and improved. Each has its own contribution; the shortcomings of one may be compensated for by the others.

If the Cubists had been correct in believing that architecture could be defined in terms of four dimensions, our means would be sufficient for a fairly complete representation of space. But architecture, as we have concluded, has more than just four dimensions. A film can represent one or two or three possible paths the observer may take through the space of a building, but space in actuality is grasped through an infinite number of paths. Moreover, it is one thing to be seated in a comfortable seat at the theater and watch actors performing; it is quite another to act for oneself on the stage of life. It is the same difference that exists between dancing and watching people dance, taking part in sport and merely being a spectator, between making love and reading love stories. There is a physical and dynamic element in grasping and evoking the fourth dimension through one's own movement through space. Not even motion pictures, so complete in other respects, possess that main spring of complete and voluntary participation, that consciousness of free movement, which we feel in the direct experience of space. Whenever a complete experience of space is to be realized, *we* must be included, *we* must feel ourselves part and measure of the architectural organism, be it an Early Christian basilica, Brunelleschi's Santo Spirito, a colonnade by Bernini or the storied stones of a medieval street. We must *ourselves* experience the sensation of standing among the *pilotis* of a Le Corbusier house, of following one of the several axes of the polyform Piazza del Quirinale, of being suspended in air on a terrace designed by Wright or of responding to the thousand visual echoes in a Borromini church.

All the techniques of representation and all the paths to architecture which do not include direct experience are pedagogically useful, of practical necessity and intellectually fruitful; but their function is no more than allusive and preparatory to that moment in which we, with everything in us that is physical and spiritual and, above all, human, enter and experience the spaces we have been studying. That is the moment of architecture.

F. Ll. Wright: Administration Building, S. C.
Johnson & Son, Inc., Racine, Wis. (1936-39).

Plate 3. Interplay of volumes as represented in photographs

F. Ll. Wright: Admin-
istration Building, S. C.
Johnson & Son, Inc., Ra-
cine, Wis. (1936-39).

61

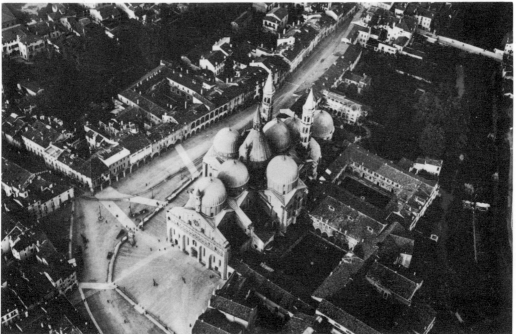

Sant'Antonio, Padua (13th-14th century).

Plate 3. Interplay of volumes as represented in photographs

St. Mark's, Venice (10th-14th century). Detail.

Plate 3. Interplay of volumes as represented in photographs

St. Mark's, Venice (10th-14th century).

Giuseppe Terragni: Children's home, Como (1936-37).

Plate 3. Interplay of volumes as represented in photographs

F. Ll. Wright: Admin-
istration Building, S. C.
Johnson & Son, Inc., Ra-
cine, Wis. (1936-39).
Detail.

Plate 4. Internal space as represented in photographs

F. Ll. Wright: Administration Building, S. C. Johnson & Son, Inc., Racine, Wis. (1936-39).

Plate 4. Internal space as represented in photographs

Piazza of St. Mark's, Venice (15th century).

F. Brunelleschi: Santo Spirito, Florence (begun 1444). Interior. See also pl. 11.

Plate 4. Internal space as represented in photographs

F. Brunelleschi: Santo Spirito, Florence (begun 1444). Interior. See also pl. 11.

Plate 4. Internal space as represented in photographs

Plate 5. Space and scale in ancient Greece

Ictinus, Callicrates and Phidias: Parthenon, Athens (447-432 B.C.).

"Basilica" (6th century B.C.) and Temple of
Poseidon (5th century B.C.), Paestum.
Views.

Plate 5. Space and scale in ancient Greece

"Basilica" (6th century B.C.) and Temple of Poseidon (5th century B.C.), Paestum. Views.

Plate 5. Space and scale in ancient Greece

71

Interior of the "Basilica" (ca. 530 B.C.).

Plate 5. Space and scale in ancient Greece

IV SPACE THROUGH THE AGES

THE HISTORY of architecture, understood in its fullest sense, is the history of the manifold determining elements which have informed building through the centuries and have embraced almost the entire gamut of human interests. Architecture has responded to such a variety of needs that to describe adequately its development would mean writing the history of civilization itself, recounting the multiplicity of factors which make up that history and showing how these factors, with the predominance now of one, now of another, have acted in concert to give rise to various conceptions of space. It would imply, moreover, an historical judgment of artistic values and of creative personalities who, on the basis of a given conception of space or of a certain taste in architecture, have produced acknowledged masterpieces, the formal content of which has become part of the architectural language and taste of the period following their own.

So far as it is possible to schematize the historical and critical analysis of a period or an artist, we can list the following factors as primary:
1) *Social premises.*   Every building is the result of a building program which is based on the economic conditions of the country and individuals who sponsor its construction, as well as on the prevailing way of life, the relations between social classes and the attendant mores.
2) *Intellectual premises.*   These differ from social premises in that they are concerned not only with what a society and an individual really are, but also with what they want to be—the world of their dreams, their social myths, religious faiths and aspirations.
3) *Technical premises.*   These refer to the progress of science in its application to handicraft and industry, and particularly to the techniques of construction and to the organization of the labor of building.
4) *Formal and esthetic ideals.*   These are the body of conceptions and interpretations of art, the plastic and architectural vocabulary, with

which the artist develops his own expressive language. In discussing taste and means of expression, all the arts have to be taken into consideration: forms which poetic fantasy may take, use of color, treatment of plastic phenomena, preference for certain types of musical figuration, fashions in interior decoration and in dress.

All these factors, not arbitrarily separated, but seen in the complexity of their mutual relationships, form the basis and background of architectural creation. In one case the supremacy of a ruling class may seem to appear as the most important element, in another case it may be a religious mythos, a community program, a technical problem or discovery, a modish fashion; but an architectural work, on the whole, is almost always the result of the balance and coincidence of all the elements which go to make up the culture from which it springs.

Once we have described these material, psychological and metaphysical premises which constitute the general configuration of a period, we can go on to the specific history of artists and their monuments. The criticism of individual works of art may be outlined in the following order:

1) *Analysis of the urban environment,* of the space surrounding a particular building and partially defined by it

2) *Analysis of the architecture,* of the spatial conception, of the way the internal spaces are experienced in a living fashion

3) *Analysis of volumetrics,* of the box formed by the enclosing walls

4) *Analysis of decorative detail,* of the chromatic and plastic elements applied to the architecture, especially to emphasize volumes

5) *Analysis of scale,* of the building proportions with reference to human scale

The reader will understand that this chapter is not intended to be any sort of history of architecture, or even the briefest of outlines, but simply a review of some of the spatial motifs that have been fundamental to the architecture of the last two millenniums. A real history of architecture would be a vast, perhaps collaborative, undertaking and would fill an important gap in contemporary culture. That such a history would be possible has been demonstrated by Nikolaus Pevsner's excellent summary and by numerous valuable monographs. The pres-

ent pages are meant to be no more than a modest, methodological contribution toward orientation in the field.

Before writing this chapter, it was necessary to decide how best to illustrate what we have just been saying: whether, on the one hand, we should exhaustively analyze a building (for example, the significant but almost unexplored subject of a Borromini church), using many drawings and photographs, with a full description of urbanistic values, spatial essence, volumetric qualities and plastic detail; or whether, on the other hand, we should briefly indicate the principal conceptions of internal space which have occurred in the history of Western architecture, leaving out some important trends and innumerable exceptions, arbitrarily taking one building as the prototype of a period. This latter method might, of course, risk being confused with the old, anti-historical system of emphasizing the features of architectural "styles," rather than specific architectural works.

The first procedure appeared safe, the second necessarily risky and full of gaps. The second procedure, however, was finally chosen, because the analysis of a single monument would have required a long critical discussion of its volumetric and plastic elements, a discussion which has been rendered unnecessary, even for the layman, thanks to numerous books by eminent scholars and to twenty years' experience by the general public in the matter and method of modern art criticism. What is still generally lacking, however, is a really unbiased education in architectural space, one free of myth and cultural "protectionism." To arrive at this, architectural criticism must follow the lead established decades ago by literary and art critics, as, indeed, by creative architects themselves in their own practice. It must rid itself of its awe of archeology and its worship of historic monuments, of an intellectual narrowness which tends to arrest the history of architecture at Valadier and the Adam brothers, as though for the last hundred years there have been no fertile minds, no artistic contributions, no spatial creations, no authentic masterpieces. For this reason it is better for our purpose to review, no matter how swiftly and unilaterally, the conception of space of various periods of Western culture from the time of Ictinus, Callicrates and Phidias to our own time and generation of architects who have gone to the school of Le Corbusier or Wright. A specialized, critical monograph would still leave unresolved the question of the general validity of the spatial interpretation we are proposing.

Space and Scale in Ancient Greece

The Greek temple is characterized on the one hand by a great lack and on the other by a supremacy which has never been rivaled. The lack consists in the ignoring of internal space; the supremacy, in the masterly application of human scale. If, throughout the course of architectural criticism, we find the admirers and denigrators of the Greek temple in constant opposition, and if in our own time we find our two most noted contemporary architects opposed in their judgments of it, this is because Le Corbusier, and those who agree with him, admire its human scale, while Wright, and those who agree with *him*, deplore its negation of space.

Anyone seeking primarily a conception of architectural space might well point to the Greek temple as a horrible example of non-architecture. Yet, whoever views the Parthenon as a giant piece of sculpture must be impressed by it as by few works of human genius. Every architect, we have seen, must also be something of a sculptor in order to extend his spatial theme to the plastic and decorative treatment of the structure, but the persistent myth that it was Phidias, the sculptor, rather than architects Ictinus and Callicrates, who conceived the Parthenon, is a perfect symbol for the purely sculptural character (and impression) of Greek religious architecture through its seven centuries of development.

In its basic elements, as every schoolboy is taught, a Greek temple consists of a raised platform from which a series of posts supports a continuous architrave which in turn supports the roof. There is also a *cella* which in the Archaic period constituted the sole nucleus of the structure (fig. 15). This had an internal space which was never developed creatively, because it had no social function. The cella was not merely an enclosed, but literally a *closed,* space and a closed or sealed

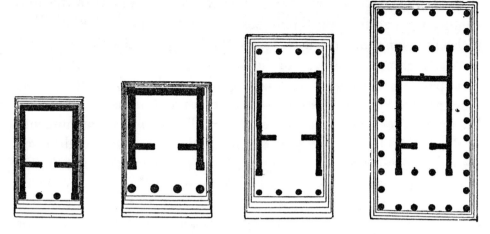

Fig. 15. The planimetric evolution of a Greek temple.

internal space is exactly characteristic of sculpture. The Greek temple was not conceived as a house of worship, but as the impenetrable sanctuary of the gods. Religious rites took place in the open, *around* the temple, and thus all the skill and fervor of the sculptor-architects were devoted to transforming the supports into sublime works of plastic art and to covering the beams, raking cornices and walls with matchless bas-reliefs (plate 5). Just as Greek thought remained remote from the psychological probing and introspection which were to become the motive force of Christian preaching and which found their first architectural expression in the dark silence of the catacombs, similarly Greek civilization was centered in out-of-doors activities, not within four walls and a roof or within the internal space of homes and temples, but in sacred precincts, on acropolises, in open-air theaters. The architectural history of the acropolis is essentially a history of urbanism, supreme in its human scale and in its unsurpassed works of serene and Apollonian sculptural grace, complete in its abstraction, remote from any social problems, self-contained in its contemplative fascination and full of a spiritual dignity never again achieved. [13]

Every architectural style corresponds to some building program and, in eclectic periods, when original ideas are lacking, architects borrow from the past motifs which are of functional or symbolic use in their buildings. Note, for instance, that Neo-Classic motifs of the 19th century were never applied for essentially architectural purposes: from Nelson's column in Trafalgar Square, London, the Lincoln Memorial, in Washington, or the façade of the British Museum, to countless rickety little porticos with their Greek columns and pediments turned out by mass production for the middle-class homes of Europe and America, the forms of Hellenic building have been called into use in monuments, in decorative details, in the plastic treatment of surfaces, and in volumetrics; but *never in architecture itself*. Generally speaking, though the Greek Revival period presents certain exceptions, the copies and repetitions of Greek style that are to be found scattered all over the world are no more than funeral masks stuck onto walled boxes having some kind of internal space. Thus they preserve all the negative features of Greek architecture without retaining the quality of human scale which distinguished the original.

Another fact is worth noting: the only part of the Greek temple in which man walks is the peristyle, the corridor between the columns and the outer wall of the cella. When the Greek temple found its way to Sicily and Southern Italy, the peristyle became broader and more spacious. This may perhaps be taken as an indication that even at that time the Italic peoples were inclined to feel spatially and to give greater importance to space, that even then they were attempting to broaden and humanize the closed formulas of their Hellenic heritage. [14]

Static Space in Ancient Rome

The architectural criteria we are applying within the limited scope of this profile of space through the ages (it is worth repeating this once again to obviate any misunderstanding) are not to be confused with esthetic judgment. The Parthenon is a non-architectural work, but it is still a masterpiece of art; and it might be said that anyone who fails to value it as a sculptural monument is failing in esthetic sensibility. If, to go on to Roman architecture, we look at reconstructions of monuments of the Imperial period and we imagine the space and feeling of the forums as they were, we may in many cases come to the conclusion that a Roman building is not a work of art, but never to the conclusion that it is not architecture. Internal space is developed on a grand scale, and if the Romans did not have the vibrant refinement of the Greek sculptor-architects, they did have the genius of builder-architects, which is, after all, the genius of architecture. Even if they were frequently unable to extend their spatial and volumetric themes plastically, these themes themselves were the product of a grand, daring and truly architectural inspiration. In fact, even those of us who are least sympathetic to Roman culture and have put up the most constant resistance to the encroachments of a Romanistic writing of history, which for nationalistic reasons would give Rome an unconditional supremacy in the history of architecture, even the most objective critics and those least interested in establishing a cultural protectionism around the products of Italian soil are unanimous in rejecting as senseless the position of certain critics who would make Roman architecture the child and servant of Greece.

The multiplicity of forms comprised in Roman building, which is in clear contrast to the unitary theme of Greek architecture; the monumental scale; the new technique of arch and vault construction, which reduced columns and trabeation to the function of decorative motifs; the feeling for large-scale volume in the reservoirs, tombs, aqueducts, arches; the powerful spatial conceptions of the basilicas and baths; the acute consciousness of setting; the fertility of invention which makes Roman architecture from the Tabularium to the Palace of Diocletian at Apalato a morphological encyclopedia of architecture; the maturation of social themes like that of the palace and the house—all these are new contributions which, absent from Greek building in spite of a partial flowering in Hellenistic times, constitute the incontestable glory of Rome, vast new horizons in architecture which were achieved at the price of the purity of style of Hellenic sculpture.

It would be easy to compare and contrast one of the Roman baths with a Greek temple and demonstrate the complete disparity between an architecture which *closes* and one which *encloses* space. But even in the monuments in which the Romans did not exploit their skill in vault constructions, even in the temples and basilicas in which they made use of the trabeated system applied in Greece, the antithesis is evident (figs. 15 and 16). If you juxtapose the plan of a Greek temple with that of a Roman basilica, you will find that what the Romans actually did was to transfer the colonnades girdling the Greek temple to the inside. Few interior colonnades are known in the architecture of Greek civilization, and where they exist, for example in the Temple of Poseidon at

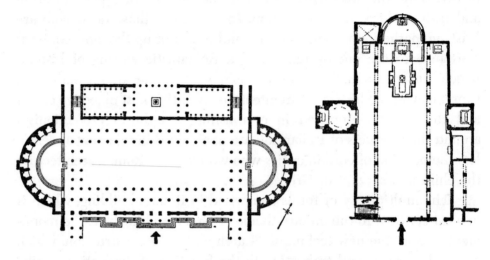

Fig. 16. Basilica Ulpia (begun 2nd century A. D.) and Santa Sabina (422–30), Rome: Plans.

Paestum, they are an answer to the structural need of supporting the roof beams and have nothing to do with any conception of internal space. In Rome, along with the technical requirements rendered more specific by the monumental scale of Imperial building, there is a social theme to the basilica, in which men live and act according to a philosophy and culture that breaks out of the abstract contemplation, the perfect equilibrium, of the Greek ideal, in order to become richer psychologically, more instrumental, more given to rhetorical symbols of grandeur. Moving the Greek colonnade into the interior means man's walking in an enclosed space, where all plastic decoration is organized toward vitalizing that space.

In the lexicon of Roman architecture, which around the close of the first century after Christ became the lexicon of the whole of European and Mediterranean civilization from Britain to Egypt, from Armenia and Mesopotamia to Spain and Timgad, it is possible to cull an infinite number of spatial motifs and suggestions. Since it included under its political control the civilizations of Asia Minor and the African coast, Rome assimilated all their architectural achievements; but the thesis of the Romanists who see in Roman forms and structures the genesis of all later spatial conceptions is no less partial and inadequate than the contrary claim sustained by certain historians who would deny Rome the merit of its spatial originality on the sole basis of some earlier and morphologically similar examples found in the Orient. The fact that the arch existed in Egypt and the vault was employed in the Orient before they came into use in Rome may be of philological interest, but from the point of view of architectural history this does not detract from the original contribution of the Romans, who used these elements in entirely different spatial conceptions, on a different scale and with different purpose and significance. Similarly, the fact that there exist in Rome cupolas and monuments similar in construction to those of the Byzantine period, of the Middle Ages and of the Renaissance does not justify the megalomania of the Romanists who are unwilling to distinguish between technique and art, or even between structural incident and spatial theme.

The fundamental characteristic of Roman space is that it was conceived statically. In both circular and rectangular spaces the rule is symmetry, an absolute autonomy with respect to neighboring spaces emphasized by thick dividing walls and a biaxial grandiosity on an inhuman and monumental scale, essentially self-contained and independent of the observer (plate 6). Today, amidst the ruins humanized by glimpses of the sky stabbing through the broken masses and by the surrounding greenery with its marble fragments scattered about as though come down to measure themselves with man, it is easy to find a romantic motif in Roman architecture; but it is a motif belonging to the ruins, not to the architecture. Essentially, official Roman building is an affirmation of authority, a symbol dominating the mass of citizens and announcing that the Empire *is*, that it embodies the force and

81

meaning of their whole lives. The scale of Roman building is the scale of that mythos, later to become reality, still later nostalgia, and it neither is, nor was it intended to be, the scale of man.

It is for this reason that when academic eclectics draw upon Roman architecture, it is not for its elements of decoration, its façades or for the invaluable lessons of its domestic buildings. The "Roman style" is used for the interiors of great American banks, for the immense marble halls of railroad stations, for works which impress us with their size, but which do not move us with their inspiration, for structures which are almost always cold and where we do not feel at home. Or else academicism has imitated Roman building whenever it has had a program of architecture-as-symbol, expressive of vain attempts at imperial revival, at myths of military and political supremacy; the result has been buildings of static spaces, rapt in the bombast of megalomania and rhetoric. [15]

Human Direction in Christian Space

Christians had to select the forms of their temple from the lexicon of Hellenistic and Roman architecture. Equally remote from Greek contemplation and self-sufficiency as from Roman taste for *mise-en-scène*, they selected from the two preceding styles those elements of which they could make vital use, marrying in their churches the human scale of the Greeks and the consciousness of interior space of the Romans. In the name of humanity they brought about a functional revolution in Latin space.

The Christian church was not a mysterious edifice which concealed the simulacrum of a god; it was not even the house of God; but rather a place of congregation, of communion, of prayer. It was logical, then, that the Christians would turn to the Roman basilica rather than to the Greek temple, because it was the basilica that represented the social, congregational theme of building. It is also natural that they tended to reduce the proportions of the Roman basilica, because a religion of introspection and love called for a humanly conceived setting, created

82

in the scale of those it was designed to receive and elevate spiritually. This was their quantitative or dimensional revolution in architecture. The *spatial* revolution consisted in ordering all elements in terms of man's path inside the church.

If we compare a Roman basilica, Trajan's for example, with one of the earliest Christian churches, such as Santa Sabina (fig. 16), we find, apart from the scale, relatively few points of difference. The Roman basilica was symmetrically disposed with respect to its two axes: colonnade opposite colonnade, apse reflecting apse. The space created had a single definite center which was a function of the building itself, not of a man's path. The Christian architect made two essential changes in this scheme: 1) he eliminated one of the apses; and 2) he shifted the entrance to the secondary side of the building. In this way he broke the double symmetry of the rectangle, leaving only the longitudinal axis, which then became the directive line for man's movement. The entire planimetric and spatial conception, and in consequence all decoration, had only one dynamic measure: the observer's trajectory through the building. It is clear that such an innovation constituted an architectural fact of tremendous importance, and it is beside the point to ransack Roman architecture in search of morphologically similar schemes (be they the basilica of Pompeii or examples of domestic building), for the Christians created a new system with old elements and gave them a new spirit and function. Imagine a visit to the Basilica of Trajan: first, you enter the lesser ambulatory; then, as you proceed, a double colonnade opens up before you so broad your eyes cannot encompass it; you feel left out, immersed in a space which has, as it were, its own *raison d'être* independent of you and which you can enter, walk through and leave, admiring but non-participating. In the church of S. Sabina (pl. 7), on the other hand, you are not left breathless by a marvel of stage-setting and rhetoric; you are able to grasp the whole of the space, which is disposed longitudinally. As you walk you are accompanied by a rhythm of columns and arches. You have a feeling that everything has been designed for the itinerary which you are following. You feel that you are an organic part of a space which has been created for you and has meaning thanks only to your presence.

The Greeks had achieved their human scale through a static proportion between the column and the height of man. The Christian world accepted and exalted the dynamic character of man; it oriented an entire building according to his path, constructing and enclosing space in the direction he was to walk through it.

The same dynamic achievement was evident in buildings planned around a single center. If we compare the Pantheon (fig. 17), that monument of Roman decadence (like the splendid edifice that goes under the name of the Temple of Minerva Medica), with the Mausoleum of

Fig. 17. Pantheon (2nd century A. D.), Nymphaeum of the Licinian Gardens, sometimes called Temple of Minerva Medica (260–68) and Mausoleum of S. Costanza (350): Plans.

S. Costanza, built in 330 A.D., the development in spatial conception will appear similar. The space of the Pantheon is static, uniformly centralized, without contrasts of light and shade, and limited by enormously massive walls. When the Empire was on the wane, when Roman philosophical thought became less extrovert and activist, and more introspective, when Roman civilization not only had been carried to the most distant shores of the ancient world, but itself taken in elements of Oriental sensibility, the Temple of Minerva Medica came into being and, in direct opposition to the preceding static concept, expanded space into imposing dark niches, enriching it with atmospheric motifs. But S. Costanza, breaking through the great niches of Minerva Medica

84

and adding a circular spatial unit, created a new spatial articulation, a dialectic of light and shade, which in Minerva Medica had merely modified the wall construction while here it characterized the space in which man was to move. It was a denial of the Roman sense of static gravity and substituted for the walls a range of marvelous paired columns which, by their radial orientation and by the linear compulsion of their trabeation, indicated to the observer, from every point of the surrounding ring, the center of the building. It is unnecessary to move around in the Pantheon, because it is a clearly defined and elementary space, taken in at first sight. Despite the variety of its structure, the Temple of Minerva Medica also does not require the observer to move around inside it. But in S. Costanza, an abundance of paths created for man, a plurality of directional indications repeated all around the space, demonstrate a new Christian achievement in buildings planned around a central point, a type of building plan which generally corresponds more to an affirmation of an autonomous architectural ideal than to a calm, rhythmic, fluent and human architecture.

Quickened and Expanded Space of the Byzantines

The theme of Early Christian basilicas was exalted and carried to the extreme of its potentialities in the Byzantine period. In the two churches of S. Apollinare at Ravenna it is evident that the Byzantine architect's problem was not of a structural nature, but of quickening and accelerating the Early Christian longitudinal scheme and giving it new urgency. In S. Sabina the arches of the nave rest solidly on columns and establish a continuity between supporting elements and those which are supported, a vertical effect that is experienced all along the axis of the church. The tempo of this Early Christian rhythm has been well described in a familiar literary image which compares its effect to jets of water spouting from and returning to the ground in a slow series of repeated arcs. In S. Apollinare this tempo becomes more intense and precipitous, negating the vertical relationship and emphasizing the horizontal. The impost blocks form a caesura between arch and column

85

at the critical center of the thrusts and create down the length of the nave a horizontal series of equidistant points, repeated beneath by the bases of the columns. The form and content of the bands of mosaic accentuate this horizontal tendency; finally, the entire chromatic revetment translates every structural passage into surface terms and substitutes for the extended, luminous planes of Early Christian architecture a fabric woven of color and scintillating with luminous reflections.

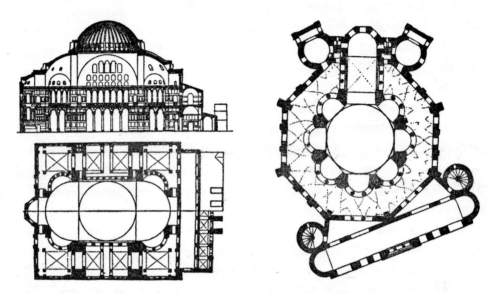

Fig. 18. Antemio di Tralle and Isidoro da Mileto: Plan and cross section of Hagia Sophia, Constantinople, (completed 537). S. Vitale, Ravenna (completed 547): Plan.

In buildings planned around a center, particularly in the great Justinian triad of SS. Sergius and Bacchus, Hagia Sophia in Constantinople and S. Vitale in Ravenna, the conception of space was basically the same. As in the longitudinally oriented basilica wherein vertical relationships are nullified and directional rhythm is accelerated to seemingly hallucinatory swiftness, so in buildings of a central plan space is agitated, as it were, into rapid currents and expanded to far distances. What do we mean by *expanded*? If you glance at the plan of Hagia Sophia (fig. 18), you will note its characteristically Byzantine configuration of enormous, semicircular, barrel-vaulted exhedras. Starting from two fixed points in the principal area, the wall surface seems to flee from the center of the building, as if thrown outwards in an elastic, centrifugal movement which opens, rarefies and expands the interior space. Even in S. Vitale, where a Latin sense of construction offers the resistance of eight robust pilasters to the soaring Neo-Platonic quality of the Eastern church, the entire spatial intent consists in expanding the octagon, denying its geometrically closed and easily apprehended form, and amplifying it indefinitely. By covering the walls with mosaics, the counterpoint of weight and support is denied, the shining and scintillating wall becomes a mantle of thin, delicate, surface material, sensitized by the propulsions and pressures of an interior space which is achieving its own concreteness in multiple, expansive bursts.

As we have indicated, Romanists have denied originality to architects of the 6th and 7th centuries and to those who followed their lead in succeeding centuries. And to prove their point, they have made much of impressive Roman experiments in spatial expansion. No one would wish to deny these experiments or challenge their statement that the Byzantines made use of them. However, the critic concerned with architectural results must recognize that the expansiveness of Roman space, as vast and as technically audacious as it was, had a final limitation in the obvious solidity of the wall structure. There is no doubt that space had been expanded, but its expansion was architecturally represented in static terms. Byzantine space, on the other hand, was not so much expanded space as space in the *process of expansion*. It contained a dynamic impulse developed in Early Christian culture; it made use of shining planes, of vast luminous surfaces, since evolved into chromatic tapestries. Just as Roman marble revetments represented a logical decorative counterpart of a static conception of space, so these tapestries signalized a new Byzantine approach.

In connection with the so-called Roman decadence, we have already taken up the Temple of Minerva Medica, which, in a psychologically tormented outburst, breaks the classical scheme with its expansiveness. But Byzantine space is free of this kind of drama; rather than a balancing out of contradictory tendencies, it is the product of a new, self-confident inspiration, which is consonant with its univocal, dogmatic and abstract spirituality.

Furthermore, comparing the Early Christian S. Costanza with the Byzantine S. Vitale, it is easy to show that these two kinds of space are not only different but opposed. We have shown how in S. Costanza the directional lines of perspective formed by the small sections of radial trabeation indicate the center of the building to the eye of the observer walking in the encircling gallery; this constitutes a centripetal motif which is clearly antithetical to the centrifugal forces of Byzantine space. And when the observer passes to the inner part of the circular space of S. Costanza, the sections of radial trabeation mark with their linear indications his passage from a luminous zone to a surrounding, enveloping, atmospheric mass. A dialectic of this sort is entirely foreign to the Byzantine conception, where it is the wall surface itself that yields and moves away from the center in concave forms, propelled more and more towards the outside, towards the peripheral space (see plan of S. Vitale) which has lost any independent architectural validity. A period in the history of space conceptions which produces monuments of this stature cannot be considered as a mere appendix to any preceding one. It bears a new message which will be heard later in the 11th and 12th centuries, in the period of St. Mark's of Venice and the Martorana of Palermo; which will echo in all of Eastern, particularly Russian, architecture; and which at the height of the Early Renaissance will even struggle to persist in the face of Italian Humanism.

The Barbarian Interruption of Space and Rhythm

In a schematic review such as this, we might be justified in skipping from the Byzantine to the Romanesque period and ignore the 8th, 9th and 10th centuries as a period of preparation which doesn't offer a spatial conception definable in terms of one or two examples. And yet our own contemporary frame of mind, perhaps because we too have gone through a long period of gestation, with a certain pleasure, is particularly akin to that of such a transition period, where we find, concealed beneath apparent decadence, courageous artists who have arrived at an entirely new statement of the architectural problem. In

Pantheon, Rome (27 B.C.; reconstructed 115-25 A.D.).

Plate 6. Static space in ancient Rome

Nymphaeum of the Licinian Gardens, also called the Temple of Minerva Medica, Rome (3rd century A.D.).

Basilica of Maxentius and
Constantine, Rome (308-12
A.D.).

Plate 6. Static space in ancient Rome

Amphitheatre, Verona (1st-3rd century A.D.).

Plate 6. Static space in ancient Rome

92

Plate 6. Static space in ancient Rome

Theatre of Marcellus, Rome (completed 12 B.C.). Model.

Dome of the Pantheon, Rome (27 B.C.; reconstructed 115-25 A.D.).

Plate 6. Static space in ancient Rome

Ruins of the Basilica Ulpia in the Forum of Trajan, Rome (2nd century A.D.).

Mausoleum of Santa Costanza, Rome (ca. 350).

Plate 7. Human direction in Christian space

Santa Sabina, Rome (422-32).

Plate 7. Human direction in Christian space

97

Plate 7. Human direction in Christian space

Santo Stefano Rotondo, Rome (468-82). Exterior view.

Santo Stefano Rotondo, Rome (468-82). Interior view.

Plate 7. Human direction in Christian space

Temple, Syracuse (5th century B.C.), transformed into a Christian church (7th century A.D.).

Plate 7. Human direction in Christian space

the historical substratum of those centuries, usually dismissed as a period of barbarism, invasion, struggle and dictatorship, a spirit of Italian independence was formed which was to triumph in the Communes. The history of the architecture of this period presents a similar situation: in apparently rude and commonplace monuments, in countless examples of minor, popular buildings, we can discern the presage and inception of Romanesque architecture, the intuition of those 11th and 12th century conceptions which represent the first renascence of architecture in Europe.

The formal and structural elements which constitute the originality of the buildings of these centuries are principally: 1) the elevation of the presbytery, as in S. Salvatore at Brescia and S. Vincenzo at Prato, Milan; 2) the addition of the ambulatory, which continues the scheme of the nave and aisles around the apse—for example, the Cathedral of Ivrea, S. Stefano at Verona, S. Sofia at Padua; 3) the increased weight of the walls and the visual accentuation of load and support, particularly evident in S. Pietro, Toscanella and in all the works of the *maestri comacini;* * and 4) the taste for rough materials—bricks, pebbles, undressed stone—used with primitive directness and great expressive effect.

In terms of space, these innovations mean first a tentative then peremptory negation of the Byzantine conception, the interruption of horizontals and the breaking of the single rhythm established by the longitudinal axis which, from the Early Christian basilica to the two churches of S. Apollinare at Ravenna, had been the principal concern of architects. Increasing the importance of the presbytery meant breaking up the length of the space. Grafting on the ambulatory meant articulating the edifice, rendering it a more complex organism at the expense of a unified spatial view. Giving the wall structure a greater feeling of weight and specific gravity and substituting rough natural materials for chromatic surfaces implied a reversal of the spatial and decorative intention of the Byzantines. There was here a return from the fluid expansionism and directional velocity of the Near East to the solid constructive sense of Latin tradition.

* *Groups of traveling master builders of the 8th, 9th and 10th centuries. Supposed to have originated in Lombardy, around Como.*

Complete emancipation from Byzantine systems of perspective and affirmation of Lombardian taste are already clearly established in S. Pietro at Toscanella. But in S. Maria in Cosmedin, Rome, a gem of those centuries, we find that within a traditional structural and figurative scheme, responding to no technical need and to no purpose other than a burgeoning, almost unconsciously felt and tentatively expressed spatial conception, an architect had the courage to break up the traditional rhythms. The elegant *élan* of the apse, the bright-colored planes which lighten the thickness of the walls with their precise linear definition, the general proportions, would enable us to classify this church as belonging to Early Christian and Byzantine tradition (pl. 9), were it not for the wall-sections, which break the continuity of the colonnades and arcades, creating a hiatus in the rhythm and scanning the space, if only timidly, into rectangular bays. This is still not an uncompromising negation of the monotonous, longitudinal theme, but only an inner dialectic, a private rebellion within this theme (fig. 19). But it is clear that the creator of S. Maria in Cosmedin, unlike his predecessors, did not

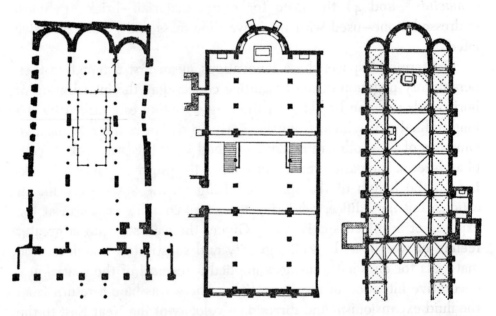

Fig. 19. Plans for S. Maria in Cosmedin, Rome (end of the 8th century); S. Miniato al Monte, Florence (1018–63) and S. Ambrogio, Milan (second half of the 11th century).

102

aim at carrying the observer along the nave at maximum and uniform speed. On the contrary, his aim was to slow down the tempo of the perspective. He impedes the directing elements. He invites you to stop at various points along the length of the church. This represents not a phase of clear awareness of spatial composition, but one of crisis in a traditional theme (cf. the Temple of Minerva Medica in relation to static Roman space), an obvious aspiration towards a new spatiality. Later, wall-sections such as those in S. Maria in Cosmedin, until then merely drawn on the surface, were to acquire new independence through being wedded to the revived technique of cross-vaulting, and were to be differentiated from the wall so as to take part in the structural organism itself, and this would mark the birth of the Romanesque period. Once its historical significance has been recognized, S. Maria in Cosmedin will become an acknowledged document of an architectural intuition and intention that anticipated modern structural logic and functional necessity, and will further confound modern Positivist and materialist historians.

Romanesque Space and Metrics

Situated at opposite ends of Europe, S. Ambrogio of Milan (pl. 9) and the Cathedral of Durham (pl. 19) represent, in the second half of the 11th century and at the beginning of the 12th, the complete realization of Romanesque ideals, which had come to maturity in the course of a century of experiment and development. Differing according to the tendencies of various countries and subdivided within each country into numerous local schools, Romanesque architecture constituted the first period after the fall of the Roman Empire when European civilization moved in harmony towards the renewal of architecture.

The kinds of medieval space we have been analyzing up to now have been basically variations on the same theme. Staid Early Christian rhythm, Byzantine acceleration, barbarian interruption of rhythm were expressions of differing aspirations within substantially similar constructive schemes. In buildings planned around a center, the bending of an Early Christian cross-section into circular form as, for example, in Rome's S. Stefano Rotondo, and the fluidity and expansion of Eastern architecture, lead, it is true, to profoundly different spatial results; but the difference is not accentuated by radical revolutions in the architectural organism itself. The Romanesque, on the other hand, was not merely a new period in the history of spatial conceptions, based on an earlier feeling for architectural voids and for the tempo of man's passage through them; it was a truly organic upheaval which followed the critical restatement of the preceding centuries of all the problems of Early Christian and Byzantine architecture by shattering that architecture and creating something integrally different.

Before the Romanesque period, the Early Christian church was a very simple structure of which we could easily make a cardboard model. All that we should need would be a few rectangular pieces for the walls, the sloping roofs, the pavement and gallery—and the whole thing would be done. The model might be made longer or shorter, at will, according to the length, breadth and number of the aisles. In a history of art where we should be seeking the unique, inimitable, poetic face of a monument, this kind of generalization would, of course, not be quite legitimate, and we should have to distinguish one early Christian basilica from another, as, for that matter, one Greek temple from another. But in this rapid sketch of spatial conceptions, we may assume that so far as the architectural organism is concerned one model will suffice for the Greek temple and another for the longitudinal basilica of Christendom up to the Romanesque period.

But try to construct a model of S. Ambrogio, of Durham, or of Cluny. Pieces of cardboard no longer suffice. It is no longer enough to enlarge or reduce the proportions of the voids, to add or subtract a column or a pilaster, to paint the walls in brilliant white or in color, to cut out larger or smaller windows or to shape simple hemispheres for the apses, exhedras and cupolas. Other means are needed to render, even schematically, Romanesque cross-vaulting, polygonal pillars, ribs and buttresses. Certainly cardboard can still be used, and heavy cardboard at that, for Romanesque wall structure is still massive; but before making the walls, it would be necessary to construct in wire the basic elements of Romanesque structure, to schematize the location and distribution of static forces. A breath would be enough to blow down our little model of the Early Christian or Byzantine church with its flat planes of non-interlocking cardboard; but in the case of our Romanesque model, its organic structure of wires grounded in the floor and rising to the ceiling, crossing the bays diagonally and returning to the floor, would defy a wind, because its elements are well knit together. The length of such a church (fig. 19) cannot be determined arbitrarily, but must be an exact multiple of the central bays; and the width of the lateral bays must be a simple fraction of the central nave.

Romanesque architecture was characterized by two features: the linking of all elements of a building and metrical space. With the first, architecture ceased to act in terms of surface and expressed itself in terms of structure; the emphasis shifted from the skin to the bony skeleton. The slow, gradual concentration of thrusts and resistance; the reduction in the thickness of walls, which through trial and error resulted in what might be called a muscular sense of membering; the final elimination of the triumphal arch, which obstructed the unity of the church; the disappearance of the atrium and the consequent increase in attention to the façades, which now expressed two-dimensionally the articulation of interior space—all these elements, in their interdependence, gave the Romanesque building the character of an organism awakening to confidence in itself and in the counterpoint of its dynamic forces, as contrasted to the inert bodies of the splendidly austere Early Christian church and the bejewelled, magnificently clothed but immobile Byzantine church. The primitive and barbaric culture of the period from the 8th century to the 10th had rent the Byzantine cloak and exposed the rude masculinity of the structural body. The body had become an organism, aware of its wholeness and its circulation; and it began to move.

The meter of Romanesque space had an exact parallel in the contemporary development of meter in poetry. The system of S. Sabina was an indefinitely prolonged *a-a-a-a-a-a;* in S. Apollinare this rhythm was accelerated to *aaaaaa;* S. Maria in Cosmedin has an articulation of *b-a-a-b,* which concerns, however, only the walls and is not expressed transversely. In S. Ambrogio, on the other hand, the system is not a simple *a-b-a-b-a*: the stress on the pilasters continuing the line of the great ribs of the nave vaults produces an *A-b-A-b-A* effect, in which the *A* becomes increasingly important in the course of time, while the *b* sinks more and more into the background. The principal significance of the Romanesque contribution lies in the fact that its interior space could no longer be discussed in terms of two dimensions; it now consisted of bay units, three-dimensional in themselves and themselves enclosing internal space. For this reason, the space and the volumetrics of the box formed by the walls are combined in a closer esthetic unity.

If man's path had a uniform cadence in the Early Christian church, became more rapid and sliding in the Byzantine church, and was slowed down by pauses which responded to purely emotional needs in S. Maria in Cosmedin; then in Romanesque structures, such as S. Ambrogio, the Cathedral of Modena, S. Zeno at Verona, the Romanesque cathedrals of France, England, Spain and all of Europe, the psychological stimuli that now guided a man's walk through a building were far more complex than a merely univocal statement of direction, as before.

Dimensional Contrast and Spatial Continuity of the Gothic

One of the commonest misconceptions about architecture would have it that the Gothic is a mere derivative of the Romanesque, the mature form toward which the 12th-century Romanesque architect vainly strove. This misunderstanding comes from a philosophical confusion of technical progress with the supposed progress of artistic values, as well as from an indifference to internal space and to the scale of buildings, which is even worse for the architectural critic.

From the point of view of construction, the Gothic architect indisputably continued, deepened and completed the experimentation begun by Romanesque architects. The designer of S. Ambrogio supported his vaults on ribs, but the fabric of the vaulting was so massive that even without ribs the vault would have remained in place. He concentrated the thrusts on pilasters, but the walls were thick enough to contain the thrusts without them. The system of organic framework was perfected by the Gothic architect: his use of the ogival arch reduced lateral thrusts; his flying arches and buttresses acted like strong arms to oppose the thrusts by themselves. The Romanesque organism thus grew more slender and more tenuous; and in the three centuries that followed, until well into the 16th century, French, English and German Gothic architecture achieved the acme of tension, becoming a bundle of bones, fiber and muscles, a structural skeleton covered by unsubstantial cartilage. In these countries, where the Gothic Style found its most complete expression and its most fevered decadence, the dream of negating walls by reducing them to their functional minimum and establishing a spatial continuity between interior and exterior appeared to have been realized. The great, storied, stained-glass windows, the fan vaults, the decorative borders of narrative sculpture and the enormous dimensions of the cathedral cancel out surfaces and planes, and reduce the entire figurative vocabulary to a dialectic of dynamic lines stretched almost to the breaking point. During the War, in several English cathedrals, bombs destroyed the stained glass of the windows and tore out the fabric between the ribs of the vaults. In these buildings, now freed even of the transparent cartilage which served as a kind of skin, it seemed as though the dream of the Gothic architect had finally come true—a dream of creating, scanning, exalting space, giving it form without interrupting its continuity.

But if this was an original aspiration of Gothic architecture, there was another more important spatial theme which distinguished it from the Romanesque. This was the bringing of dimensional forces into contrast. For the first time in the history of Christian church architecture, and indeed for the first time in the general history of architecture, architects conceived spaces which were in deliberate antithesis to human scale, which induced in the observer not a sense of peaceful contemplation but a mood of imbalance, of conflicting impulses and emotions, of struggle.

We have already spoken of the opposition between human and monumental scale. Modern feeling for space, which we shall analyze at the end of this chapter, has been greatly conditioned by this problem.

We are well able to distinguish a building conceived and constructed for man from one built as the symbol of an idea, a myth, to impress itself upon and dominate him. Modern science has given us a tool for going deeper into the analysis of these spaces, where, to use a common phrase, "we don't feel at home." The difference we have established, up to this point, has been of a quantitative and psychological nature; every building has been qualified by the relationship between its dimensions and the dimensions of man, and, therefore, greatly to change this relationship in reproduction has always resulted in farce or bombast. Reduced to half its size, a Greek temple becomes a toy; blown up to twice its size, it becomes one of the innumerable, repulsive products of Neo-Hellenism.

Scale, however, has an additional meaning, which concerns not the proportional relations between man and building, but the proportions within the building itself and their effect on man. In all of Western architecture up to the Romanesque, these proportions have been expressed in two ways: 1) by the equilibrium of directional tendencies; or 2) by the predominance of one directional tendency over all the others. Perfect equilibrium is to be found in Greek temples and in Christian buildings of a central plan. We find the predominance of a single tendency (vertical direction), for example, in the Egyptian temples at Karnak and Luxor (pl. 19), or in the Byzantine basilica (horizontal direction). In the Gothic, on the other hand, two directions, the vertical and the longitudinal, coexist in silent but acute antithesis. The eye is drawn by two opposite indications, attracted by two themes, two kinds of space. The spatial history of Gothic cathedrals throughout Europe, the distinctions among national and regional schools, the individual physiognomy of single monuments, are based principally on the varying intensity of this contrast in direction (pl. 10). Of primary importance is the relationship between the rectangle of the cross-section and the rectangle of the plan; the relationship between man and these two rectangles is of secondary importance.

If we compare Italian, French and English Gothic (figs. 20 and 21), we find that this directional contrast becomes more and more accentuated as we move north. In the Cathedral of Milan with its five aisles,

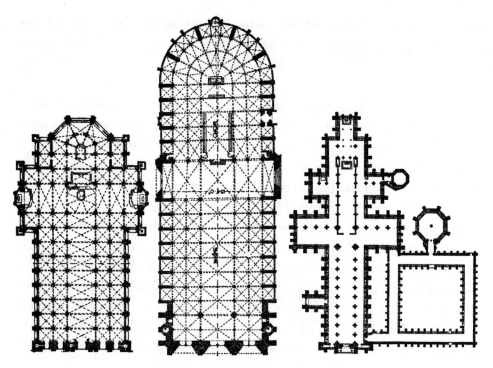

Fig. 20. Cathedral of Milan (begun 1386); Notre Dame, Paris (1163–1235) and Cathedral of Salisbury (1220–58): Plans.

Fig. 21. Cathedral of Milan, Cathedral of Reims (1212–41) and Westminster Abbey (1245–69): Cross sections.

the width is still far greater than the height: the longitudinal tendency is predominant and the vertical direction so subordinate that the space —despite the ogival arches, the clustered pilasters, the tracery, the triumphal accompaniment of gargoyles and pinnacles, in short, all the iconographic trademarks of the "style"—is closer to classical equilibrium than to Gothic drama. In French Gothic, heights are abruptly increased, but the five aisles are often retained, as in Notre Dame of Paris and in the Cathedral of Bourges. In cathedrals having only three aisles, such as at Amiens, rows of chapels are added, or aisles go around the apse in wide ambulatories, resulting in a circular movement which gives a final emphasis to the longitudinal direction by connecting the two sides of the church. But in the great cathedrals of medieval England at Ely, Salisbury, Worcester, Lichfield and Westminster, the two directional motifs appear simultaneous and of equal value: the longitudinal tendencies break at right angles in the presbyteries or in the terminal chapels; there are never more than three aisles; and thus width, as a dimensional factor, disappears before the competition of the other two dimensions. In the linear decoration of pillars, fan-vaults and triforiums, English architects achieved a negation of planes and surfaces, a nervously agitated treatment exceeding anything found in the cathedrals of Reims or Chartres, or in Sainte-Chapelle of Paris.

As we have said before, carrying a spatial theme to its utmost possibilities through technical acrobatics and decorative ecstasies does not mean creating a more beautiful architecture. We may prefer Notre Dame to Salisbury, as we may feel closer to a Romanesque church than to a Gothic cathedral, but this is a matter of taste, personal preference and individual judgment. Our present concern is simply to establish the spatial language of each period, the culture out of which individual monuments emerged with their own esthetic features.

English Gothic architecture, besides possessing the characteristics mentioned, had an entirely modern quality, which we might call *organic*: that of expansion, of the possibility of growth, of the joining of buildings. While the Cathedral of Milan and Notre Dame of Paris are isolated constructions, the English cathedrals are often integrally connected with a series of buildings, are extended in them and in turn dominate them. The same characteristic is also seen in other types of buildings, such as monasteries, castles and houses. This reflected the narrative character of medieval architecture and town planning, which was like a continuous tale told by individuals of successive generations, freely varied and episodic, but unified by a profound linguistic bond. It was in direct opposition to the single, isolated statements of classical conception, to the minor and major axes which divided a city into orthogonal grids, and to all those buildings, regardless of period, whose sole value lay in the beauty of the ensemble, permitting neither subtraction nor addition. In a word, it was opposed to all those static forms, which, however aglow with ideas and personalities, did not express the rich, vital process of historical progression.

Laws and Measures of Early Renaissance Space

The first volume of a two-volume history of art always closes with the Gothic, the second opening with the Renaissance. This practical classification has created in the mind of the general public a gulf in historical continuity which critics have vainly attempted to bridge and which is particularly out of place in the history of architecture. The 15th century saw the discovery of America, the discovery of perspective and the printing press; but not the discovery of Renaissance architecture, whose origins go back to the 11th and 12th centuries, and are present and continuing throughout the Middle Ages. Not only do monuments such as the Portico of Civita Castellana, the church of the SS. Apostoli and S. Miniato in Florence [16] testify to the birth of Renaissance culture before 1400, but the very sense and direction of 13th- and 14th-century architecture in Italy anticipate the new humanistic attitude. This is particularly true if we consider it from the point of view of the dimensional contrasts of the Gothic, which, as we have seen, were very slight in Italy. The Cistercian Order created a belt of Gothic influence which crossed Italy diagonally from Vercelli in Piedmont to Apulia and along which a number of monuments were constructed under foreign architects. At the same time, however, Italian schools were developing not only in southern centers, rooted in the splendor of Arab-Norman architecture, and in Venice, where independent themes were evolved, but also in Tuscany and on the Mediterranean coast, so rich in works of art and so fertile culturally that they deserve more than customary marginal treatment in histories of the Gothic period.

Even a cursory view of Italian structures of the 14th century will resolve the question of the continuity from Romanesque to Gothic and then to Renaissance architecture. The myth of Brunelleschi ending the 14th century with the dome of S. Maria del Fiore and beginning the 15th with the Portico degli Innocenti, like so many other myths, has no basis in the concrete facts of architectural history. Parenthetically, we might recall that other myths regarding the classicism, or worse, the Romanism, of the Renaissance are no more than summary and ambiguous hints at far more complex realities. For a long time the Renaissance has been the subject of two antithetical conceptions: according to one, the Renaissance was an absolute novelty with respect to the preceding period and so can not be brought into historical framework; the other conception reduces the Renaissance to a "neo-ism," a revival of Roman architecture, depriving it of any claim to creative vitality. Modern criticism, in order to correct these two popular misconceptions, has had to work in two opposite directions—vindicating both the originality of the Renaissance and its perfectly logical place in the historical succession of Western culture.

What then is the new element which makes its appearance with Brunelleschi in 15th-century architecture? It is essentially a mathematical conception developed from Romanesque and Gothic metrics: the search for an order, a law, a discipline opposed to the incommensurability, infinitude and dispersion of Gothic space, and to the casualness of Romanesque space. S. Lorenzo and S. Spirito would not be very different in spatial feeling from certain Romanesque churches were it not for the fact that, apart from any reasons of construction or correspondence between bays and vaults, these churches have a spatial measurement based on elementary mathematical relationships. In terms of space, the thought and humanism of the 15th century may be summed up by this experience: if you were to enter S. Lorenzo or S. Spirito, in a matter of a few seconds, whether or not you are familiar with the metrical law involved, you could fully measure their internal space, so governed are they both by that readily grasped law.

112

From a psychological and spiritual point of view, this represented a radical departure. Up to then it was space which determined the tempo of man's progress through a building, which led his eye along the path willed by the architect. With Brunelleschi, for the first time, it was no longer the building that took possession of the observer, but the observer who, by apprehending the simple law governing its space, possessed the secret of the building. Those who speak of medieval transcendentalism and Renaissance immanence are making literary allusion to the fact that in the Renaissance man was no longer propelled by Early Christian rhythm, carried away by the perspective flights of the Byzantine period, drawn by the slow and shadowy succession of Romanesque bays, or excited and tormented by the mystic heights and longitudinal violence of the Gothic style. In S. Lorenzo he moves about with the clear feeling of being at home in a house constructed by an architect who has not been swept away by religious exaltation but rather pursues rational, human methods that hold no mysteries, at ease in a house conveying the calm precision of the humanly universal. An analogous feeling of serene equilibrium was offered by the relationship between sculpture and man in the human scale of the Greek temple; and it is no accident that those, like Ruskin and Frank Lloyd Wright, who are out of sympathy with Greece, should also be hostile to the Italian Renaissance. But the great achievement of the 15th century was to transfer the human feeling which animated the Greek temple to the field of interior space or, more exactly, to translate into spatial terms the metrics which in the Romanesque and Gothic periods had been limited to the plans.

Superficial observers accuse the Renaissance of a mere nostalgic imitation of past culture, whereas it was actually the cradle of the most advanced modern research and experiment. Our liberal objection to anything which weighs upon man, dominating and oppressing him; our present day rejection of monumental architecture as such; our social axiom of the city planned for man; our conception of the house in terms of modern material, psychological and religious needs—all of these immanent, organic, spiritual attitudes of ours can be traced in a direct line of descent from the architecture of the 15th century, because it was precisely then that the foundation was laid for the modern architectural idea: that it is man who establishes the law for architecture, not *vice versa*. The entire effort of the Renaissance consisted in emphasizing man's intellectual control of architectural space; and we who find ourselves, after a contorted eclecticism and a too-long self-criticism, trying

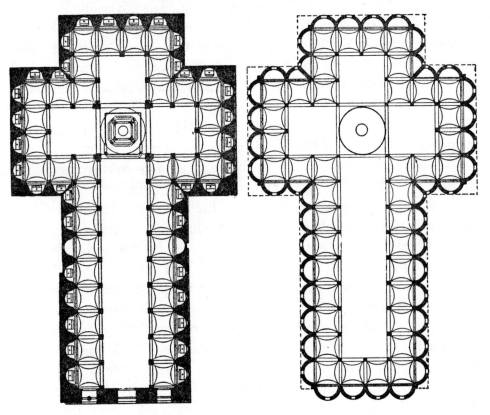

Fig. 22. Brunelleschi: S. Spirito, Florence (begun 1436). Actual plan and original plan.

to create a period in which culture and individual vision might be profoundly unified, in which the personal, creative moment and the hour of social reflection might be intimately joined, turn precisely to 15th-century culture because there we find a "new science," an integration of art and thought, creativity, doctrine and genius. There the logical, almost mathematical, substratum never had become merely mechanically produced, but prepared a solid base for a common spatial vocabulary which inspired and stimulated, rather than inhibited, individual expression.

In the light of this intellectual stimulation, it was natural that 15th-century architects should revise traditional schemes of spatial organization. In S. Lorenzo, Brunelleschi's measurement of space meant constructing according to simple mathematical relationships. But in S. Spirito he went further, extending the metrical system through the entire church, making the transept conform to the nave and aisles and extending the longitudinal scheme beyond the transept. In addition, he closed the spatial metrics circularly, continuing the aisles around the apse and, in the original plan (unfortunately not carried out), along the entrance wall. To achieve complete control of his space and to unify his conception Brunelleschi found it necessary to minimize the importance of the longitudinal axis and to create a circular movement around the cupola. A number of other new features of 15th-century architecture can be similarly explained and justified as replying to the same spatial needs.

It is logical that a central rather than a longitudinal plan should correspond better with a unitary conception of space. We have seen that the Early Christian and Byzantine aim was to provide a dynamic force, even in buildings of a central plan. Now we find the opposite: a program for rationally *controlling* all the dynamic energies inherent in axes. In the 15th and 16th centuries, buildings of a central plan were preferred, the abundant examples ranging from S. Sebastiano in Mantua to Bramante's and Michelangelo's projects for St. Peter's. In the Latin-cross schemes, the long arm is shortened; whenever possible preference is given to the Greek-cross plan, where the arms balance each other—the composition does not *culminate* in a center, but *spreads out* from the center under the dome, and it is from here that the aisles radiate. The little side-aisles of the Christian basilica created marginal shadows, undefined areas antithetical to the new urge of dominating everything intellectually. Accordingly Alberti, in S. Andrea, Mantua, eliminated the side-aisles and created a single space by enlarging the central nave and lining it with rows of chapels. A single path, a single idea, a single law, a single unit of measure—this was the human and humanistic, the classic, but never classicistic, will of Renaissance architecture.

We find the same thing in the treatment of walls. Every decorative factor of medieval dispersion was eliminated. The two-color scheme of Brunelleschi's work in contrast to the rich palette of 13th-century surfaces was as sharp and challenging then as is Functionalism's abolition of decoration today, compared with the architectural ornamentation of the 19th century.

Medieval palaces have rough surfaces in which windows are casual elements placed without compositional order, preferably asymmetrical openings repeating on the surfaces the sculptural decoration of the triforiums. The windows are, in fact, arranged so as not to interrupt the chromatic planes of the walls. The walls, in turn, are acted upon by the commanding lines of the cornices, which break the vertical lines and extend the perspective beyond the volume of the building to infinity. Perfectly coherent with the spatial themes of the Gothic period that followed, this conception was absolutely contrary to Renaissance culture, which set up against this desire to open and "unfocus" vistas, the imperative will to define, to measure, to establish a law, even for surfaces. Now, beside Palazzo Strozzi, which rationalized but did not revolutionize medieval forms, Alberti built Palazzo Rucellai, the first to divide and measure a volumetric surface with pilasters, and to establish a rhythm according to simple modules. What Brunelleschi had wrought in interior space, Alberti accomplished for surfaces.

And now what about the "execrated" applied decoration? Certainly it is this decoration which was to be exploited throughout the 19th century in all the Italianate villas from the United States to Russia, and against which modern architecture was to direct its barbs. But this applied decoration, however lifeless and academic in the hands of its imitators, corresponded in the 15th century to the spatial theme of its time and provided a measured rhythm on the walls as a complement to the inspired construction of measured, metric voids; applied decoration in the Renaissance was an act of profound coherency and so of integral, cultural and artistic validity.

Sant'Apollinare Nuovo, Ravenna (493-526).

Plate 8. Quickened and expanded space of the Byzantines

San Vitale, Ravenna (530-47).

Plate 8. Quickened and expanded space of the Byzantines

119

San Vitale, Ravenna (530-47).

Plate 8. Quickened and expanded space of the Byzantines

Antemio di Tralle and Isidoro di Mileto: Hagia Sofia, Constantinople (completed 537).

Antemio di Tralle and Isidoro di Mileto: Hagia Sofia, Constantinople (completed 537).

Plate 8. Quickened and expanded space of the Byzantines

121

Antemio di Tralle and Isidoro
di Mileto: Hagia Sofia, Constantinople.

Plate 8. Quickened and expanded space of the Byzantines

122

Sant'Ambrogio, Milan (second half of the 11th century).

Plate 9. The Barbarian interruption of space and rhythm and Romanesque space and metrics

Cathedral of Mächtige. Soffits.

Santa Maria in Cosmedin, Rome (7th-8th century).

Plate 9. The Barbarian interruption of space and rhythm and Romanesque space and metrics

125

San Miniato al Monte, Florence (1018-63).

Plate 9. The Barbarian interruption of space and rhythm and Romanesque space and metrics

San Zeno, Verona (12th-13th century). View of the interior.

San Zeno, Verona (12th-13th century). Detail.

Plate 9. The Barbarian interruption of space and rhythm and Romanesque space and metrics

127

Buscheto and Rainaldo: Cathedral of Pisa
(1063-12th century). Diotisalvi: Baptistry of
Pisa (1153-1399). Bonanno: Leaning Tower
of Pisa (1173).

Plate 9. The Barbarian interruption of space and rhythm and Romanesque space and metrics

16th-Century Plastic and Volumetric Themes

The basic spatial themes initiated in the *quattrocento* were continued in the century following and, through works of great genius, were enriched with volumetric and decorative motifs of such diversity and individuality that any attempt to summarize them briefly would be futile.

The cultural and archeological tendencies which—along with an illusory belief in the possibility of finding a valid rule for absolute beauty—had already appeared in Alberti and his school, in the 15th century, prevailed in the ideology of 16th-century treatises, where we find affirmations of such flat-footed classicistic conformity that to take them literally would be to regard them in the same light as we regard 19th-century Neo-Classic academicisms. But there is a difference between the mentality of our time and that of the 16th century. After having shattered all previous rules and conventions, we now invoke a criterion of absolute originality and critically attempt to search it out even in artistic production of secondary importance. Architects of the 16th century—or at least those among them who were true artists—even when they created in perfect freedom, trampled classic canons underfoot with sublime indifference and had the false modesty, the hypocrisy or the cultural shrewdness to pay seemingly unconditional homage to classical antiquity, declaring themselves humble followers of ancient architectural ideals. There is thus a clear dichotomy between cultural theory and creative practice, which, though later to become the forerunner of Neo-Classic scholasticism and intellectual justification of innumerable eclecticisms, did not, in the Renaissance, weaken the vital force of that series of supreme artists from Bramante to Palladio.

From the point of view of its spatial themes, the 16th century, as we have said, developed further the centralizing aspirations of the preceding century, a vision of space as absolute, easily grasped from any visual angle and expressed in the eurhythmic balance of proportions. The "Golden Age," the *cinquecento*, embodied 15th-century ideals, but reincarnated its forms with a plasticity which, barely latent in Brunelleschi and more fully realized in Alberti, now triumphed in a multiplicity of variations on the basic theme of symmetrical space.

Bramante's *Tempietto* at S. Pietro in Montorio, Rome, inaugurated the 16th century and may perhaps be regarded as a declaration of its principles: absolute centrality, maximum value placed on dimensional relationship between the various parts of a building (the proportions, in other words) and solid plasticity (pl. 12). This little temple is a kind of 16th-century Parthenon and as such shares all the merits and defects of that Hellenic masterpiece. The analogy between Greece and the 16th century does not, however, go beyond this common formal ideal; Renaissance architectonics called for *internal* space.

If the Gothic had aimed at continuous and infinite space disappearing down the length of its vistas, the Early Renaissance had not enclosed space so much as had given it a rational, metric order that rendered it readily definable and measurable. Now the 16th century qualified the same spatial research in eurhythmic terms, returning to the old antitheses between interior and exterior space with the heavy and corporeal solidity of its walls and the massive plasticity of its decorative elements. The specific character of 16th-century architecture was therefore manifested not so much in a renewal of spatial conceptions as in a new sense of volumetrics, of the static and formal balance of masses within which the 15th-century spatial dialectic took on new color and meaning, and was reinforced and rendered massive by the new taste which preferred a rounded whole and a consistent, often monumental, solidity to a line or a chromatic plane.

In accordance with this new taste, all the visual, dynamic directives of earlier periods were excluded. If a Gothic tower drew the eye upward toward its spire, if a Christian basilica set the tempo of man's path through a building, if a 15th-century palace and courtyard indicated in the slenderness of their membering and in their delight in linear effects a circular, visual itinerary within a symmetrical scheme, then in the 16th century all dynamic forces, previously subdued but not spent, were finally put to rest. A range of 15th-century arcades, even if linked together by a mathematical law of composition, shows movement through a continuous inner vibration of lines of force; but a range of 16th-century arcades stands in weighty and motionless equilibrium. The planimetric, spatial, volumetric and decorative articulation of an edifice was no longer the expressed process of its architectural conception, but a statement, almost a command, which organized and dominated the whole. Roman motifs of static space were wedded to the 15th-century law of composition, qualifying without obliterating it.

The difference between 15th- and 16th-century styles is well illustrated by the classic comparison of the dome of S. Maria del Fiore, the Cathedral of Florence, with that of St. Peter's, Rome. In the Florentine

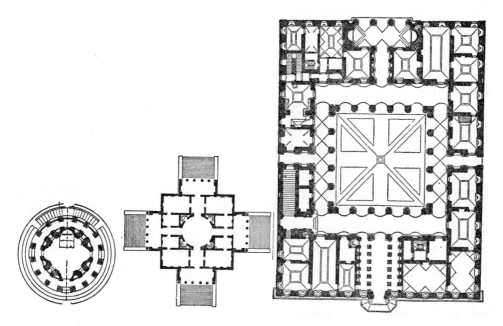

Fig. 23. Bramante: *Tempietto* at S. Pietro in Montorio, Rome (1503). Palladio: Villa Capra, Vicenza (1550) and A. da Sangallo: Palazzo Farnese, Rome. Plans.

work the Gothic ideal of infinite space is expressed in the counterposition of prominent linear ribs and neutral zones which fill the webbing of the dome; the Renaissance conception of measured space, on the other hand, is manifested in its clear division into eight sections, which articulate and link the whole together according to a simple, elementary law. In the dome of St. Peter's the ribs are doubled in number and the webbing is no longer a neutral zone. There is not even a memory left of that dynamic antithesis between the lines of force and the walls, which Brunelleschi had preserved, though giving it a rational order;

Michelangelo made ribs and webbing combine to form a powerful plastic mass. It is thus natural that Brunelleschi's dome, resting lightly on a previously constructed drum, should have no weight, that without being tied to the church it should rise out of it in a self-sufficient equilibrium; and that Michelangelo's dome (particularly in original projects, which had it much lower than the present one) should penetrate into the body of the basilica, sink into it, because of the drum, weighted by the reinforcing paired columns, which, instead of articulating and separating, bear down with static insistence. In Michelangelo's mind the great effect of St. Peter's depended on the relationship between the mass of the dome and the mass of the church, in other words, on massive volumetric values.

Similarly, in conceiving palaces, the Middle Ages expressed the Gothic ideal of continuous space, now in the big airy loggias, now in the pictorial surface treatment of the building-box, which through rustication was permeated with an intense play of light and shade, while the openings were loaded with elaborate plastic decoration with a consequent lack of clear distinction between solids and voids. This ideal is maintained in the Early Renaissance, in rationally ordered form in Palazzo Strozzi and articulated in linear units in Palazzo Rucellai (both shown in plate 11). The 16th-century architect emphasized unitary volume and massive gravity in a palace, either with the prominence of solids over voids, as in Palazzo Farnese (pl. 2), or with superimposed orders, a translation into plastic terms of those linear pilasters we have seen in Palazzo Rucellai.

With the disappearance of linear directives, volume and plasticity came to the fore. Just as the horizontal terminating line of a medieval palace was crenellated—and so properly speaking was not a terminal line, but an area of contact between solid and void, between building and sky—by the same token the mighty cornice of Michelangelo's Palazzo Farnese suggests meaningful weight and accentuates the break between exterior and interior space.

In the criticism of *cinquecento* architecture it is all too easy to fall into misunderstanding; this desire for the static, the corporeal, the rounded whole, is by no means to be confused with the static space of

132

ancient Romans. Roman space, to be sure, had its imitators in the 16th century, but these, insofar as they were mere imitators, fall outside the history of art. In the authentic poets of the period the aspiration toward symmetry, the centric ideal of the rotunda, the taste for "fleshy" materials, is never separate from that body of measured laws which had been the profound study of the early 15th century; it is for this reason that their work is solid and grave, but never inert. In some cases, within the same general plastic and volumetric framework, they are, indeed, light and joyous. It is enough to think of Palladio's villas, which humanize the undulating plains around Vicenza with a beauty free of any archeological nostalgia.

Movement and Interpenetration of Baroque Space

Michelangelo did not initiate the Baroque period, as so many histories of art continue to repeat. He embodied the drama of the second half of the 16th century, which aimed at giving movement to the closed staticity of Renaissance space, but did not carry the effort to the breaking point. The relationship between Vignola, Michelangelo and Borromini is not unlike that between the Pantheon, Minerva Medica and S. Costanza. Minerva Medica represents a romantic rendering of closed Roman space; Michelangelo, an agitation of the contents of the 16th-century walled-box. The entrance to the Laurentian Library in Florence (pl. 12) is the archetype of Michelangelo's work: its giant orders no longer fit quietly into the walls or the volume, but are a plastic symbol of the need to open, enlarge, disrupt and burst them. The mounting steps break into and dominate the small space as though calling for revolt against its static stereometry. But just as the architect of Minerva Medica was not yet able to create a new Christian sense of space and had to limit himself to working away part of the walls enclosing traditional space, so Michelangelo, the sculptor, could not abandon *cinquecento* space in favor of a totally new theme, but altered and subverted its walls and volumes and provided one of the most dramatic moments in the history of architecture. Once he had brought wall-structure to a crisis, he stopped. But he opened the way to Baroque space.

Baroque is the liberation of space. It is mental revolt from the rules of treatises, from convention, elementary geometry and immobility. It is liberation from symmetry and from the antithesis between interior and exterior space. Because of this spirit of liberation, the term *Baroque* has taken on a psychological meaning, which, beyond its specific application to 16th- and 17th-century architecture, refers even today to an attitude of freedom, a creative state of mind disengaged from intellectual and formal preconceptions, a condition common to more than one moment in the history of the arts. Thus we speak of a Hellenistic Baroque and a Roman Baroque (the period during the late Empire when architects criticized the solidity of closed Roman space), and there is even talk of a Modern Baroque in the Organic Movement's declaration of independence from the Functionalist schemes and formulas of the 1930's.

Here, of course, we are not using the term in the generic sense of moral revolt (in which sense, indeed, it runs the risk of being confused with Romanticism), but in its specifically architectonic or spatial meaning; for obviously the features that characterize 17th- and 18th-century space are not to be found in those other periods, which, by illegitimate extension of the word, are called Baroque.

The age-old hostile criticism directed against the Baroque has never been aimed at Bernini and his school. Despite the fact that the fortress-like, closed-box structure of Palazzo Farnese was followed by the open and inviting Palazzo Barberini with its illusions of perspective and its large windows; that after the centric schemes of the 16th century, austere in their formal self-sufficiency, the colonnade of St. Peter's opens its arms to receive crowds of the faithful; despite even a taste for *mise-en-scène,* the entrance of naturalistic elements into building, the sculptural and architectonic motives which inundate the parks of the great villas, and the consequent polyphonic union of exterior and interior space—all of this never irritated the critics, partly, no doubt, because Palladio, who was deified by the scholastic classicists throughout Europe, was too free a genius to adhere strictly to the rules which he himself had so greatly helped establish.

134

Critics and laymen have never carried to its conclusion their protest against the introduction of dialectics into 16th-century space, and its liberation, by the school of Bernini. Essentially, Bernini respected the classic sense of space, though he gave its components movement and tension. In Bernini's S. Andrea al Quirinale, the substitution of an ellipse for a circle, even though the ellipse is a more dynamic form, did not bother anyone so long as all the elements around this heretical figure were organized according to *cinquecento* principles. No one has

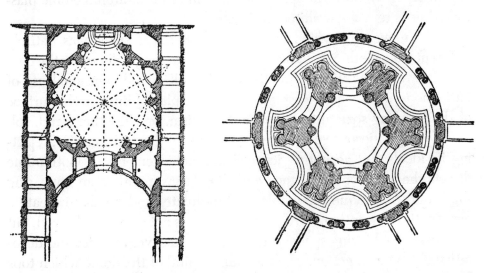

Fig. 24. Borromini: S. Ivo alla Sapienza, Rome (completed 1662). Plan of the church and plan of the dome.

ever, with any deep conviction, hurled anathema at a Pietro da Cortona, a Vanvitelli or numerous other minor artists whose inventively fertile palaces, churches and fountains brought light and splendor to the austere streets and squares of the 16th century.

The point at which critics—and even now large sectors of public opinion—have balked, is where the Baroque ceased to limit itself to bringing the light of new taste to old schemes, but created a new conception of space, that is to say, precisely where the Baroque was at its greatest. Borromini and Neumann: it was over these two commanding figures of international Baroque that swords crossed. Even nowadays, understanding Baroque architecture does not only mean freeing the mind from classicist conformism, accepting daring, fantasy, variability, intolerance of formalistic canons, variety of theatrical effects, asymmetry, disorder, the symphonic collaboration of architecture, sculpture, painting, gardening and *jeux d'eaux;* it means all this, certainly, but principally it means understanding Baroque space; it means, to cite only the examples illustrated in plate 13, admiring S. Carlino alle Quattro Fontane, the interior of S. Ivo alla Sapienza and the Vierzehnheiligen. In these supreme monuments the Baroque character of movement and interpenetration triumphed not only in terms of architectonic plasticity but in terms of architectural space.

The movement which characterized Baroque space was entirely different from Gothic dynamism. The latter was engendered by the contrast between two visual directives and made two-dimensional use of indications of perspective established by the play of lines on the surface of the building structure. Baroque dynamism, on the other hand, followed the plastic and volumetric experience of the 16th century, rejecting its ideals, but accepting its technical achievements. A Gothic line directs the eye along a surface and thus keeps a wall from appearing solid, but in Baroque the whole wall undulates and bends to create a new spatial conception. Baroque movement is not a space achieved, but a *process* of achieving space; it represents space, volumetrics and decorative elements *in action*. The ascending spiral of the dome which tops Borromini's S. Ivo alla Sapienza is its plastic symbol.

In terms of space, this movement implies the absolute negation of any clear and rhythmical division of voids into geometric patterns. The juxtaposition of contrasting spatial figures and their horizontal (fig. 24) or vertical (fig. 25) interpenetration, deprive each form of a fixed prismatic or stereometric identity. It is virtually impossible to conceive the shape of S. Carlino from its plan. On the side of the entrance there is a half oval; there is another in the apsidal space; and there are parts of two ovals in the chapels to the right and to the left. These four geometric segments meet and penetrate one another in a planimetric composition which has retained nothing of the clear scansion and eurhythmic metrics of the Renaissance. As for altimetry, where a 16th-century architect would have kept building and dome entirely distinct

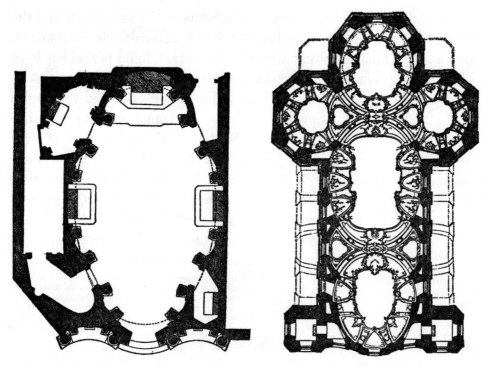

Fig. 25. Borromini: S. Carlino alle Quattro Fontane (1640). Neumann: Vierzehn-heiligen, Main (1743–72). Plans.

from each other, as two contraposed volumes, Borromini conceived the whole space as a single unit: the ellipse of the dome is fused in a single continuum with the space beneath, and the wall structure is modelled so as to accentuate and carry to an extreme this interpenetration of spatial figures with a continuity of plastic treatment. In the Neumann church, begun in 1734, the dome was abolished altogether in order to avoid, by absorbing their dynamism, extraneous elements that might throw the play of spatial interpenetration out of focus. Three ovals of different size follow each other in the nave without any break in continuity; to these are added two circles, which correspond to what was formerly the transept. However, to achieve a more dramatic space, the focal point is placed not at the crossing of the two arms (as under the dome of earlier churches), but in the middle of the central oval, where Neumann has set his altar. As though this were not enough, there is also a rudimentary second transept consisting of two supplementary altars, which form a spatial connection between the first ellipse and the principal ellipse. The whole is clothed in spectacular decoration and enlivened by an astonishing play of light. In fact, in no period has light been used to such an architectural advantage as in the Baroque.

Besides masterpieces like these, the period admittedly includes examples of paradox, empty license, bombastic theatricality. But understanding architecture means being able in dealing with periods of rigid spatial language, such as the Renaissance, to see the point where individual spirit expresses itself and achieves a poetic language which rises above architectonic rules of syntax and semantics. It means, in periods of revolt like the Baroque, knowing how to distinguish works with disorder as an end in itself from works of genius, which achieve a moment of classical synthesis even if by means of an infinite multiplication of images (pl. 14).

Urbanistic Space of the 19th Century

The Baroque period was followed by the Neo-Classic period and by 19th-century Eclecticism with its numerous revivals in which a soggy literary Romanticism was married to scientific archeology. From the point of view of interior space, the 19th century offered variations in taste but no new conceptions. It was a period of mediocrity of invention, marked by a dearth of genuine poetry. Its history includes noble buildings and a number of real artists: John Nash in England, Gabriel in France, Valadier in Italy; but in the present summary we have of necessity neglected so many great architects of the past that we shall not be tempted to discuss these personalities, though they have the special attraction of being true architects in a period of little creativity. As they accomplished nothing essentially new in terms of space, their works are readily understandable in terms of spatial conceptions already discussed.

The small, middle-class house, which was one of the principal building themes of the late 19th century and the beginning of the 20th, represented, as a whole, a total failure in terms of inner space and

138

therefore of architectural interest. This type of structure was nothing but a small-scale version of the classical, monumental palace. The old, grandiose, static rooms here became cubicles, statically juxtaposed, but without a sense of grandiosity; if late Renaissance buildings occasionally erred on the side of the rhetorical, late 19th-century houses were generally stunted, tightly closed, miserable, mean. Whether their windows imitated the Gothic or the Romanesque, whether their little porches had Greek caryatids or twisted Baroque columns, whether their appearance was artfully ruin-like, archaic or rendered "mysterious" by Gothic gargoyles, they almost always remained phantoms: their stylistic differences were strictly a matter of decoration, varying with chaotic changes in the romantic current or with the piecemeal whimsy of a client, easily satisfied by an architect who was by now capable of everything, and nothing. When all this is judged in terms of space, it is necessarily found wanting. None the less, compared with much of today's commercial construction, many 19th-century buildings seem to have an enviable coherency as well as a certain dignity. In this sense, in fact, the 19th century is entitled to an apology for our attitude towards it.

The true virtue of 19th-century architecture, however, is in its exterior space, in its town planning. Following the grandiose phenomena which resulted from the industrial revolution—principally new means of locomotion and mass migration to the towns—the 19th century, forced into problems of urban space, erupted beyond ancient city walls, created outlying districts, formulated social themes of urbanism in the modern sense of the word and built garden cities. The importance of this contribution has been so decisive that if we were writing not of architecture, but of city planning, a field in which the public has urgent need of guidance, this 19th century, against which historians and critics inveigh, would perhaps be our greatest chapter in the history of exterior space. In this connection we must add that as we come closer to modern architecture, the distinction which we have established, for purely practical reasons, between interior and exterior space, and which in the third chapter we have already cautioned the reader to regard as relative, appears still more arbitrary.

If a monument out of its proper context is like a picture with an offensive and disproportionate frame, if the exterior of a church like S. Maria in Cosmedin loses all meaning after razing the structures in front of it, if the colossal, urbanistic blunder of demolishing the Spina dei Borghi deprived Bernini's Colonnade of its scale, the dependence of architecture on town planning—indeed, their virtual identity—is even more evident in our own period. Our trivial building regulations, our flat and uniform zoning, our lack of volumetric and spatial imagination in town planning, are reflected directly in architecture to the extent that they often impede the creation of good architecture.

The innumerable modern ant-hill developments, those upper-middle-class apartment houses which have mushroomed around our big cities—even if we can isolate two or three buildings by real architects—seem far more desolate, oppressive and anonymous than a 19th-century quarter in London or a number of garden cities built at the beginning of this century. There an absence of good architecture is at least compensated for by an urbanistic order, a desire for organization stimulated by something nobler than megalomania and commercial speculation. If nothing else, the 19th century attempted to curb the disastrous turn that urbanization had taken. It clarified the problems and suggested the first solutions of the modern city.

Organic Space of Our Time

The ideals, history and achievements of modern architecture have been exhaustively expounded by Pevsner, Behrendt and Giedion. For Italy the author has summarized them in an earlier work, *Towards an Organic Architecture,* and later integrated them in *Storia dell'Architettura Moderna.* Here, it will suffice to point out the specific features of modern space.

It is based on the *open plan.* Social needs no longer set grandiose and monumental themes for architecture, but rather the problem of a home for middle-class families, of a dwelling for workers and farmers who until now have lived in suffocating little row-cubicles. These needs plus the new technique of construction in steel and reinforced concrete, which make it possible to concentrate elements of static support in a slender skeletal framework, provide the practical conditions for realizing the theory of the *free* or *open plan*. Most people have seen a reinforced-concrete or steel-framed house under construction: supporting pillars and floors are raised from the foundations to the roof before any interior or exterior walls are put up. Eclectic architecture had timidly masked this crystalline structure with an ancient wall system in imita-

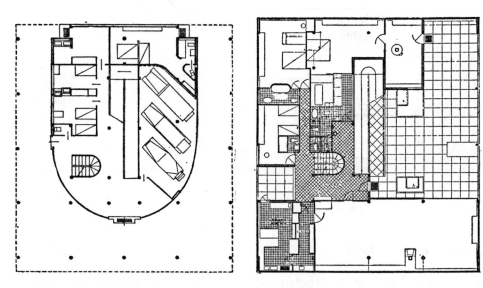

Fig. 26. Le Corbusier: Villa Savoie, Poissy (1928–30).

tion of the solidity and plastic consistency so favored by the 16th century. Modern architecture, on the other hand, has attained the spatial dream of the Gothic by making good use of new technics, by executing its artistic insights with greater precision and audacity. Using vast windows, by now entire walls of glass, it has established complete continuity between interior and exterior space.

Internal wall partitions, which no longer serve static bearing functions, may now be thin, curved, freely movable. This creates the possibility of linking up interior spaces, of joining together the numerous cubicles of the 19th century, of passing from the static plan of the traditional house to the free, open and elastic plan of modern building.

Even in the average house the living room is merged with the dining room and study, the entry is reduced to add space to the living room, the bedroom becomes smaller, service areas are designed to make more breathing space for that large articulated area where the family lives: the living room. If this can occur in urban buildings, forced as they are into a mold of commercial standardization and bound by the restrictions of town zoning, the open plan offers unlimited possibilities in an isolated building of elastic, internal divisions and subdivisions, either

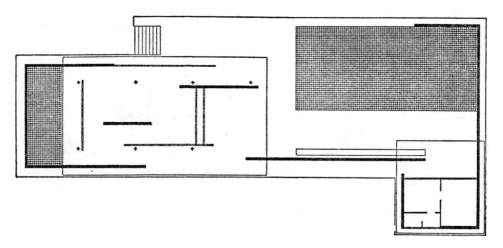

Fig. 27. Mies van der Rohe: Pavilion, Barcelona (1929).

within a rather frozen structure (figs. 26 and 27) or by means of the structure itself (fig. 28).

Modern space, therefore, re-evokes the Gothic desire for spatial continuity and incorporeal structure, not as a final goal, however dynamic, but as the result of a dynamic social process. It makes use of Baroque experimentation with undulating walls and volumetric movement, though here too not because of definitive esthetic ideals, but as a consequence of functional considerations which are soon absorbed and forgotten in splendid poetic forms, in which massive Baroque walls are replaced by light, suspended partitions of glass or some thin insulating material. In many industrial and community buildings, such as schools and hospitals, modern architecture resumes the spatial metrics of the Renaissance and resurrects Renaissance taste for patterns of scan-

142

sion, which are translated into terms of modern building needs. Within the framework of social needs, modern technique and taste—partly in polemic opposition to 19th-century applied ornamentation—call for simplicity and reduction of figurative elements to the minimum. Many earlier achievements in space recurring in modern architecture thus take on a new artistic physiognomy. The contemporary movement, moreover, has continued the richly individual expression of Renaissance and Baroque examples. To the general public it may "all look alike," because our cities are so infested with pseudo-modern, which has nothing modern about it except an irrelevant and cliché "freedom from decoration." In reality, the contemporary movement is differentiated from one country to another and within each country has as great a variety of masters and schools as the most fertile periods of history have had.

The two most important conceptions of space in modern architecture are those of Functionalism (occasionally called the International Style) and the Organic Movement. Both international by now, the first began in America with the Chicago School of 1880-90, but found its fullest formulation in Europe and its leader in the Swiss-French architect, Le Corbusier. The second has its greatest exponent in the American genius, Frank Lloyd Wright, and only in the last decade has it taken firm hold in Europe. Although these two conceptions have in common the theme of the open plan, they interpret it in different ways; the first strictly rationally, the second organically and with a full sense of humanity.

Among the masterpieces of contemporary residential architecture, the Villa Savoie of Le Corbusier (pl. 15) and Falling Water by Wright (pl. 16) show clearly the difference in their manner of composition and therefore in their poetic approach. Le Corbusier starts with a reticulated structure, a quadrangle measured regularly by pilasters. Within a rational, geometric formula his space is enclosed by four walls with continuous windows. It is only at this point that we begin to deal with the problem of the open plan. The partitions are not static, but formed by thin movable walls. On the second floor there is a large terrace, and the exterior and interior space meet at a glass wall which can be opened

143

completely. In vertical terms, a continuity between the floors is established by a wide ramp which cuts through the building, rising as far as the terrace of the top floor. All of this is carried out with perfect freedom, but within a precise stereometric scheme.

In Mies van der Rohe's delightful pavilion constructed for the Barcelona Exposition of 1929, the order of the structural elements remains rigidly geometrical, but the architectural volume is broken up (fig. 27). The continuous space is cut by vertical planes which never form closed, geometrically static areas, but create an uninterrupted flow in the succession of visual angles. Here we have a still freer development of the modern theme.[17]

In the case of Wright, aspiration toward spatial continuity has a far more expansive vitality: his architecture is centered around the living reality of interior space and is therefore in opposition to elementary volumetric forms (pl. 2), to that sense of proud detachment from nature characteristic of Le Corbusier. For Wright the open plan is not a dialectic carried on within an architectural volume, but the final result of a conquest expressed in spatial terms, starting from a central nucleus and projecting voids in all directions. It follows that the resulting drama of volumetrics has an audacity and richness undreamed of by the Functionalists, and its very insistence on decorative elements indicates, quite apart from their sometimes doubtful taste, a desire for freedom from the bare, self-flagellating severity of early European rationalism.

Both in America and Europe functional architecture met the mechanical needs of an industrial civilization. For this reason it waved

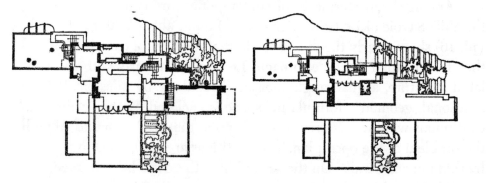

Fig. 28. F. Ll. Wright: Falling Water, Bear Run, Penna. (1936).

144

Westminster Abbey, London
(12th-14th century).

Amiens Cathedral (1220-88).

Plate 10. Dimensional contrast and spatial continuity of the Gothic

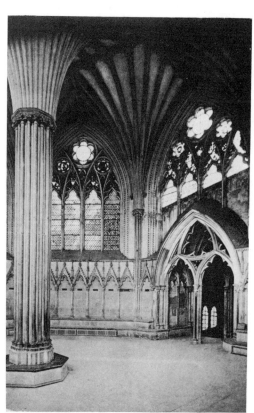

Chapel, Cathedral of Wells
(1180-1425).

Chapel, King's College, Cambridge (1441).

Interior of the tower, Strasbourg Cathedral (completed 1439).

Plate 10. Dimensional contrast and spatial continuity of the Gothic

Abbazia, Casamari (completed 1217).
Detail of a pilaster.

Plate 10. Dimensional contrast and spatial continuity of the Gothic

Abbazia, San Galgano (1227-
88). Detail of a pilaster.

147

Plate 10. Dimensional contrast and spatial continuity of the Gothic

Cathedral of Milan (1386-1401). Seen from
a side nave.

Palazzo Vecchio, Florence (begun 1299). See also pl. 17.

Plate 11. Laws and measures of early Renaissance space

149

L. B. Alberti: Palazzo Rucellai, Florence (1447-51).

Benedetto da Maiano: Palazzo Strozzi, Florence (begun 1489).

Plate 11. Laws and measures of early Renaissance space

F. Brunelleschi: Santo Spirito, Florence (begun 1444). See also pl. 4.

Plate 11. Laws and measures of early Renaissance space

F. Brunelleschi: Interior of Pazzi Chapel, Florence (1429-43).

Bramante: *Tempietto* at S. Pietro in Montorio, Rome (1503).

Plate 12. 16th century plastic and volumetric themes

Palladio: Palazzo Chiericati, Vicenza (1551).

Plate 12. 16th century plastic and volumetric themes

154

Plate 12. 16th century plastic and volumetric themes

Michelangelo: Laurentian Library, Florence (1524-26).

Michelangelo: Laurentian Library, Florence (1524-26).

Plate 12. 16th century plastic and volumetric themes

156

the flag of utility, that is, conformity to the practical function of a building and to the technics employed, and proclaimed the slogan of "the house for the average man," standardized and anonymous. Organic architecture, represented in America by Wright and in Europe by Aalto and by Swedish and younger Italian architects, satisfies more complex needs and functions; it is functional not only in technics and utility, but also in terms of human psychology. It bears a post-functionalist message which speaks of the humanization of architecture.

Because of this message, organic architecture has been erroneously interpreted as a "Romantic" movement, and some have even spoken of the inevitability of a modern Baroque period following functionalist rationalism. In an entirely superficial simplification of history, it has been said that just as the Greek temples of the Periclean period (rationalist) were followed by the Hellenistic (Baroque), the monuments of the Roman Empire (rationalist) by the Baroque of the Roman decadence, the Romanesque (rationalist) by the Gothic (romantic), Renaissance intellectualism by the Baroque of the 17th and 18th centuries, and the Neo-Classic by the romantic movements of the 19th century— so by a law of history, functionalist rationalism is destined to be followed by organic romanticism. Actually, this reasoning is entirely capricious and does not take into account a fact which is not romantic, but scientific: the rise of modern psychology.

The often-repeated functionalist formula of the "machine for living" echoes a naive, mechanical interpretation of science as fixed, logically demonstrable, mathematically indisputable and invariable truth. This is an old interpretation of science which has been replaced in our time by a more relative, elastic, articulated concept. Today's scientific spirit throws light on the entire field of the irrational in man, uncovering individual and social problems of the unconscious. Architecture, which in the course of twenty years of Functionalism has brought itself up to date with respect to the science and technology of the last century and a half, is now broadening and humanizing itself, not in romantic reaction, but through the natural progress of scientific thought. If problems of town planning for the working masses engage the Functionalists in a heroic struggle for the minimum house, for the standardization and industrialization of building, in other words, if the Functionalists are concentrated on the resolution of *quantitative* problems, then it is organic architecture which recognizes that man has dignity, personality, spiritual meaning, and realizes that the problem of architecture is as much *qualitative* as quantitative.

Organic space is rich with movement, directional invitations and illusions of perspective, lively and brilliant invention (pl. 3). Its movement is original in that it does not aim at dazzling visual effects, but at expressing the action itself of man's life within it. The Organic Movement is not merely a current in taste or an anti-stereometric and anti-prismatic vision of space, but is aimed at creating spaces which are not only beautiful in themselves, but represent the organic life of the people who live in them.

Although the criterion of esthetic value, to be sure, is no different for contemporary work than for that of the past, the artistic ideal of modern architecture is inseparable from its social setting. An undulating wall is no longer undulated purely in response to a poetic vision, but to better accompany a movement, a path taken by man. Organic architecture's use of an ornamentation which plays on the juxtaposition of different materials (plaster next to wood, reinforced concrete next to stone and glass), a new sense of color, a new joyousness in contrast to the cold severity of Functionalism, is determined by deeper psychological insight. Man in the diversity of his activities and life, in his material and psychological needs, in his spiritual nature, the whole man, whose body and soul are vitally integrated, is the cultural center for contemporary art.

This social, collective and individual imperative that is now guiding and inspiring modern town planning and architecture in its functionalist origin and organic development, is not to be interpreted as a materialistic or merely practical exigency. In effect it is a great religious movement, not inferior in force and suggestion to the religious and spiritual movements which inspired the spatial conceptions of the past, a movement which is immanent in aim because it is human, but which goes beyond problems of circumstantial comfort to face the life and death problems of a society in which the individual craves freedom and

158

seeks passionately for an integration of his culture. It is a movement which in this atomic age and in the name of a happier and more productive future for man launches an appeal for a harmonious physical environment, for a town planning and an architecture which will be the sign and promise, or at least the comfort, of our civilization.

For this reason, too, we find again in organic space that quality of the English Gothic which is anti-classicist in the sense that it does not seek to constrain man in a building defined in terms of fixed, immutable canons, where the only beauty is that of the totality, but aims at glorifying the organic character of growth, of variety and often of description.[18] It is also for this reason that human scale is the fundamental law in the organic conception of architecture, which rejects all building that dominates man and is independent of him.

This brief review of the history of spatial conceptions thus ends with a contemporary social comment and, indeed, commitment, which is relevant to our subject since modern architecture has achieved concrete reality in works of art worthy of being ranked with the masterpieces of the past.

V INTERPRETATIONS OF ARCHITECTURE

A HISTORY, written according to modern critical standards, of the various interpretations of architecture from early Greek conceptions and Vitruvius to Wölfflin, Mumford and Giedion, would fill a volume in itself. The greatest difficulty in compiling a history of architectural criticism is that to a large extent the most inspired insights into architecture are to be found scattered throughout books on philosophy and esthetics, in poems, novels, stories and in the notebooks of architects. True critics of architecture are rare and, as the bibliography at the end of this book indicates, they are usually committed to abstract problems of composition, or engaged in the ancient battle between Greek and Gothic, between the classic "impersonal, universal idea" and romantic "individual expression," between the formal and static, the picturesque and mobile. Nothing is said about interior space, and often there is not even an indirect suggestion of its reality. Yet, when we turn to historians, philosophers and estheticians, again and again we find acute and penetrating observations as, for example, the following passage from Focillon:

"The profound originality of architecture as such rests in the internal mass. By giving definite form to this hollow space, architecture creates its own universe. Doubtlessly external volumes and their profiles interpose a new, entirely human element on the horizon of natural forms to which conformity and harmony always add something of the unexpected; but, if you think of it, the greater wonder is the conception and creation of a kind of reversal of space. Man moves and acts on the exterior of every object; he is always outside, and to go beyond surfaces, he must break into them. The unique privilege of architecture, among all the arts, whether in creating houses, churches or interiors, is not to shelter a convenient emptiness, but to construct an interior world in which space and light are measured according to laws of geometry,

160

of mechanics and optics, that are necessarily implicit in the natural order of things, but are not used by nature herself."

Here Focillon hits the mark, even if he subsequently wanders from it, as when he concludes that *"the builder does not envelop a void but rather a definite dwelling-place of forms, and, working on space, he models it from outside and inside like a sculptor."* In other words, Focillon runs the risk of confusing the hollow sculptural mass, the envelope of space, with interior space itself.

The method adopted by some writers, like Borisavljević, cannot produce a living history of architectural criticism, for they first expound their own theory and then judge other theories according to their agreement with the hypotheses of their own previously stated one. The method should be empirical, experimental; it should be developed in terms of concrete examples, approving and condemning on the basis of tested facts. For instance, despite the brevity of our own survey, we have shown a collection of some of the principal monuments from the Greek period to the present day, in the sixteen plates thus far provided. In the illustrations below (pls. 17-20) we offer twenty more works selected at random along the course of past centuries; together with the preceding examples they allow for a variety sufficient to test the validity of any interpretation of architecture. For an interpretation to make any sense, it must illuminate a permanent aspect of architecture; it must demonstrate its effectiveness in illustrating every work, aside from whether or not it covers comprehensively all aspects of the given work. Only in this way shall we be able to distinguish *interpretations* of architecture from *critical fallacies* and make clear that these fallacies derive from generalizations of poetic particulars, from illegitimate expansions upon elements characterizing a single figurative world.

To state, for example, that the Cathedral of Wells (pl. 10) is determined architecturally by the technical construction of its ogival arches, flying buttresses and umbrella vaults is a mistake only to the extent that the term *determined* is given exclusive meaning, as if progress in engineering were enough in itself to explain Gothic art. But if it were put that new building techniques *contributed* to making the Cathedral of Wells possible, this statement would be correct. A technical interpre-

161

tation is thus an authentic interpretation, applicable to all monuments of architecture. Of course, it is more meaningful in certain periods, such as that of the Greek (pl. 5), the Gothic (pl. 10) and modern Functionalism (pl. 15), whereas it embraces only secondary aspects of the Christian (pl. 7), the Renaissance (pl. 12) or the modern Organic Movement (pl. 16). However, we do not consider this interpretation a *fallacy*, since it contains in its grasp a permanent element of architecture.

If, instead, we were to consider one of Belcher's theses, that of static truth, according to which it is necessary, in order to obtain a sense of firmness, for the lower part of a building to show greater solidity than the upper, we must ask ourselves whether this too is an *interpretation*. We must conclude that it is obviously a *fallacy*, because it lays down a law that is not observed by all the buildings illustrated here. In the architectural conceptions of the Renaissance in Florence this law is often valid, and striking examples of its operation may be seen in the Palazzo Riccardi and the Palazzo Quaratesi, where rusticated walls lighten gradually as they rise; but the fallacy consists in the generalization, in elevating a poetic particular to the value of a principle which applies neither to medieval palaces with their uniform chromatic surfaces, nor to Palazzo Strozzi or Palazzo Rucellai and even less to modern architecture with its suspended volumes (pls. 15 and 16).

In the opening of the preceding chapter we schematized cultural themes that fostered creative works and personalities. Geoffrey Scott, in his masterpiece, *The Architecture of Humanism,* enumerates and discusses many aspects of architectonic culture and, finding them insufficiently comprehensive, terms them *fallacies.* They are not, however, fallacies: they are aspects of the cosmos of the work of art, and they characterize it. To write a technical, political, psychological or scientific history of architecture remains legitimate and useful; we go astray only if we presume that these partial histories of some aspects of architecture are complete histories—without any qualifying or limiting adjective—of architecture.

Now, then, what is the relationship between our spatial interpretation and other interpretations of architecture? Does it include them all, summarize some of them, or is it just one more interpreta-

162

tion among many, though perhaps the most important of them all?

In replying to these questions it will be opportune to review briefly the principal interpretations current, which, as we shall see, fall fundamentally into three categories: interpretations of content (first six, below), physiological and psychological interpretations (seventh) and formalistic interpretations (eighth). We shall give examples of each.

Political Interpretation

Almost all handbooks of architectural history recapitulate, either at the beginning or during a description of particular monuments, salient factors in the political life of the various periods. Some, however, like to establish a close dependence of architecture on political events:

—When was the golden age of Greek architecture? The 5th century B.C. (pl. 5). Why? Because Athens had won the Battle of Marathon in 490, the naval engagement of Salamis in 480 and the clash at Plataea the year after. It was then that the age of Pericles had become a splendid one: first in political performance, then, or consequently, in architectural achievement.

—How is the impulse of Gothic building in France and England to be explained? By the rise of nationalism and the fervor of the Crusades. In England, under Henry III, the cathedrals of Lincoln, Salisbury and Westminster (pl. 10) were founded. In France, under Louis IX, Amiens and Chartres, Reims and Beauvais and Sainte-Chapelle were erected.

—Perpendicular Gothic is an English style (pl. 10) which has no parallel on the Continent. Why? Because in the 15th century, under Henry V, England faced the problem of its internal policy and came to terms with Scotland and Wales. The ripening of a purely English period in the arts corresponded to isolationism in English foreign policy. Scarcely did England, under Henry VIII, inaugurate a new foreign policy, consequently coming into contact with Europe, when the Renaissance crossed the Channel and had the effrontery to set an Italianate tomb within the very heart of the Gothic style: the Chapel of Henry VIII at Westminster.

—In 1453 the Turks occupied Constantinople and a vast band of Byzantine artists emigrated to Europe and England. They carried with them their age-old familiarity with oriental domes. And behold, after three hundred years of Gothic spires and belfries, there reappear on British soil the first domes, heralding a type which will later crown St. Paul's in London.

—The reaction against Rococo architecture that took place in France towards the middle of the 18th century also had its roots in politics: the Rococo had been the style of the aristocratic salon and, as such, after the Revolution, was destroyed in the name of classical ideals.

—In 1933, the Nazis came to power in Germany and this determined the end of the Bauhaus (pl. 20). This political fact caused the emigration of modern German architects to England and this is why, under the impulse of Gropius and Mendelsohn, the functionalist movement developed in that country.

—Why is it that despite the presence of so many talented men, modern architecture in Italy cannot be compared with French and German schools prior to Hitler? Because in Italy the Fascist regime favored a rhetorical-monumental trend rather than a rationalist direction. And why was it that at a certain moment even the clique headed by Marcello Piacentini, who provided a pseudo-modern mask for classicistic megalomania, was obliged to adopt the most shamelessly academic device of arches and columns, as in the buildings for the Rome Exposition of 1942? Again, because of a political fact: the alliance of Italy with Germany and the consequent obscurantist influence of Nazi culture.

As we have seen, then, political interpretation concerns the causes of architectural currents or the symbolism of its styles: that the Palace of Stupinigi (pl. 14) is a symbol of aristocratic reaction, and that Mendelsohn's Schocken Store (pl. 19) is a symbol of capitalist democracy. (We shall go into the question of symbols at greater length below.)

Philosophical-Religious Interpretation

This interpretation states: "Architecture is the visual aspect of history;" that is, the way in which history appears. Such an interpretation can be given on the level both of politics and of philosophical conceptions:

—The Protestant Reformation marked the final hour of Gothic architecture in England and the advent of the Renaissance. It is because of the Reformation that Somerset could destroy the monastic buildings of Westminster and build a house for himself out of the remains, or that innumerable churches could be transformed into schools and castles. The English Protestants leagued themselves with German and Dutch Lutherans, and that is why—long before Inigo Jones undertook his Palladian tour of Italy at the beginning of the 17th century—the Renaissance arrived in England in German and Dutch versions. Without the Reformation, we should not have had the fifty-two churches of Wren, the splendors of St. Stephen's in London and of Hampton Court; we should not have had a Georgian civilization with its Protestant starkness.

—Neo-Platonism, formulating a concept of the infinite, broke with the vision of being as an isolated phenomenon. This philosophical direction was reflected in the architecture of the Hellenistic period and explains its revolt against the volumetric and plastic isolation of the Greek temple (pl. 5), and its new emphasis on stage effects.

—It is too easy to say that Gothic architecture reflected the monastic spirit. That may be true of Chartres, but at Amiens a profane atmosphere speaks of the accord that had been reached between the good (spiritual) life and good living.

—If the Renaissance signified the triumph of the non-clerical or of Protestantism, it is natural for the Church of Rome to have rebelled and encouraged Baroque architecture (pl. 13) with its pomp so antithetical to humanist austerity (pls. 11 and 12).

—When particularized, fragmentary, pagan religion was suc-

165

ceeded by the universalistic conception of Stoic philosophy, architecture passed from the static solidity of the Pantheon to the space of the old Roman Baroque (pl. 6).

This philosophical-religious interpretation of architecture may be further divided into two parts: (a) symbolism and (b) historical phenomena that involved architectural culture.

Scientific Interpretation

A particular aspect of scientific positivism tends to underscore parallels between mathematical and geometric conceptions and architectonic thought:

—Euclidean geometry, shaping the sentient being according to specific measurable dimensions, went hand in hand with Greek spatial sensitivity (pl. 5).

—In Brunelleschi's conception (pl. 11 and fig. 22) we find a desire to set symmetrical planes and plastic accents along the central axis of the buildings, where there are generally rarefied atmospheric voids. He knew only the rules of central perspective; this explains his insistence on the median axis.

—The law governing space in the Renaissance resulted from perspective, from the possibility of objectively fixing a three-dimensional body. The philosophy of individualism and immanence of the 15th century derived from this new science of space, which permitted the projection of a building on paper, "as man sees it."

—Architectural training was not enough for constructing the dome of San Lorenzo in Turin (pl. 14). Mathematical knowledge was needed in addition; if Leibnitz had not discovered integral calculus, and if scientists had not been intent on contriving methods of descriptive geometry, architect Guarini could never have created it.

—Without the fourth dimension of Cubism, it would never have occurred to Le Corbusier to suspend the Villa Savoie on piles (pl. 15), or to make all four façades of the building equal, thus destroying the distinction between main, lateral and rear elevations that was implicit in perspective representation, where every element was hierarchically coordinated with respect to a predetermined point of view. The same cubist discovery was accompanied by the decline of Euclidean geometry, by the revolution in modern physics which, counter to Newton's static conception, conceived space as relative to a moving point of reference. Without the pronouncement of modern mathematics on the convergence of the two entities of space and time, without Einstein's contribution to the concept of simultaneity, Cubism, Neo-Plasticism, Constructivism, Futurism and their derivatives would not have emerged.

Economic-Social Interpretation

"Architecture is the autobiography of economic systems and of social institutions"—this is the thesis of another branch of positivist opinion:

—What was medieval architecture? It had its foundation in the agricultural economy of the village, in the system of group sharing and of guilds, in the practical needs of defence. That is why we find similar architectural forms appearing whenever similar economic conditions appear. The constructions of New England colonists were not very different from those of medieval European civilization: the same variety of motifs, the same characteristics of organic growth, the same considerations of defence pervade two periods with a similar economy, despite a lapse of centuries between them.

—What was Renaissance architecture? The product of the dissolution of the medieval village, of the displacement of economy from farm to sea, of the prevailing of fishing, industry and commerce over agriculture, of the consequent breakup of communal conscience which accompanied the formation of economic classes. Even among workers, the guild was broken up and the individual architect born. To put it as an equation, Peter Harrison was to Brunelleschi as the end of the American agricultural economy was to the end of the European agricultural economy. How is it to be explained that the Renaissance started in Italy in the 15th century, reached England after two centuries, and America after three? And why did it last three or four centuries in Europe, while it survived for less than a hundred years in America? Because the forces working for the disbandment of the village and the forces working for the development of a mercantile civilization went into operation in the various countries at different times and for varying periods. Architectural forms followed: 15th-century Italian architecture was light and joyous, and the same may be said of the architecture of American colonists. Brunelleschi was anti-chromatic; American Georgian was white. Both of these architectural styles observed the rules yet avoided monotony.

—What did 16th-century classicism correspond to? To a process of economic stabilization in which we find a landed oligarchy maintaining all its feudal privileges without the social responsibilities implicit in medieval economy, and, alongside it, a merchant class that had lost its original spirit of enterprise and now, feeling "heroic" and noble, erected dwellings with the scale and severity of public buildings. Italian palaces of the 16th century had their counterpart in the Virginia and Maryland manor houses, in the plantation houses modelled on Roman villas. Just as princes of the 15th and 16th centuries in Europe were at the same time statesmen, savants and artists, so in America Thomas Jefferson reflected the same aristocratic versatility. The myth of a Caesar who gave his name to a city appeared again with Washington; the formal town planning of the Renaissance was reincarnated in Major L'Enfant.

—What was eclecticism? The architecture of industrial expansion. When conflict arose between utility and life, between myth and art, two aspects of industrial civilization appear: romanticism, turned toward the past, and mechanicism, turned toward the

future. Exotic curiosity, mimicry and comfort are the characteristics of every eclectic period. Accordingly, there is no fundamental
difference between the eclecticism of the 1st and 2nd centuries A.D.,
that of England at the end of the 18th century, and that of America
in the second half of the 19th century.

    —In its heaviest, most static and severe forms, classicism was
the architecture of the economic phase that goes under the name
of imperialism. It was, as Lewis Mumford puts it, the architecture
of compensation, offering magniloquent stones to a people from
whom it has taken bread and sun and everything worthy of man.
It was the architecture of Henry VIII and Elizabeth at the beginning of the British Empire, of Louis XIV and Napoleon III, of
Hitler and Mussolini. What difference does it make if the ancient
Romans expressed their imperialism by building roads, while the
Americans, between 1893 and 1910, constructed railroads? What
distinction is there between Le Nôtre and Haussmann, the architects of the Chicago Columbian Exposition and the authors of the
Rome Exposition of 1942? They all betrayed life and progress in
favor of shams, imitations and decorative cosmetics: the first betrayed the Baroque; the second the school of Richardson and Sullivan; the third the rationalist movement.

    The economic-social interpretation also has its symbolistic applica-
tions. Isn't the dome of the Capitol in Washington—a hemisphere set
on a drum of equidistant columns—a symbol of a sovereign law over-
riding the equality of all citizens? And aren't the skyscrapers of New
York (pl. 17) the symbol of a satanic individualism, of the power of the
trusts, casting a shadow on all the buildings around them?

Materialist Interpretations

    Secondary positivistic interpretations are legion. One of these
maintains that architectonic morphology can be explained by the geographic and geological conditions of the places where particular monuments are situated:

—Interior space does not exist in the Greek temple (fig. 15), because the mild climate allowed religious ceremonies to take place out of doors.

—In Egypt the roofs are flat, in Greece and Rome they are slightly pitched, but the pitch becomes steeper as you go north to England and Norway.

—Granite in Egypt permitted the creation of large-scale statuary and decoration, but not of the refined Hellenic modelling that can be achieved only in marble. In the same way, the chromatic effects of Babylonian, Assyrian and Persian architecture are to be explained by the use of brick and terracotta, and that this is true is further proved by the fact that we find them again as a distinctive characteristic in far later times, in Belgium and Holland. Wood has affected Scandinavian architecture from remote eras down to Aalto and the present.

So far as building materials are concerned, it should be noted that architects and critics seem to favor the facile approach of determinism. When Frank Lloyd Wright had to choose a title for a book covering his work from 1887 to 1941, didn't he propose *In the Nature of Materials*? Many critics in seeking to defend modern architecture begin by speaking of reinforced concrete and steel. Even Lewis Mumford, observing that Neo-Hellenism emerged earlier in America than in Edinburgh or Paris, has offered for consideration that Greek forms, having had their morphological origin in wooden construction, adapted themselves better to a country abundantly supplied with timber.

This kind of interpretation is extended by some authors to cover the broadest and most arbitrary contingencies:

—Why did the Gothic endure for so long in the northern countries, while it took hold only briefly in the southern regions? Because in the south the sun's rays fall almost perpendicularly and so greater shadow contrasts are obtained with cornices and horizontal projections, but in northern countries the sun is lower and its rays more tangential, and accordingly vertical lines are more effective in the use of light as an architectural instrument.

—Why do we find an abundance of romantic, picturesque and informal architecture in the north, while in the south we observe an insistence on classicism? For a similar reason: in the north light effects are not subtle enough to emphasize minute elements of design, while the luminous reflections of the south vivify and give independent expression to every example of the monotonous Greek building pattern.

Ruskin established his rules of architecture according to the nature of the terrain: if the terrain is cultivated and smooth, a purely functional architecture of simple forms is called for; if it is cultivated and gay, or wooded, picturesque architecture is indicated. If the sky is serene, architecture should be horizontal; if it is gray and cloudy, as in the north, architecture should be vertical and linear.

The utilitarian interpretation is well known: every building should correspond to its purpose. The debate begins, however, when an attempt is made to specify the nature of the purpose. We need not insist on the purpose of the Monument of Lysicrates, the Column of Trajan or any of the examples of sculptural architecture illustrated in Plate 1, that is, buildings without interior space. But what is the purpose of the Taj Mahal (pl. 17), if it is not that of a pure and eternal tribute of love from a man to a woman? The utilitarian interpretation makes sense only if its horizons are extended to include the psychological and spiritual.

Another aspect of positivism bases itself on archeological research to explain the development of architecture from the 15th century on:

—When did the Italian Renaissance begin? After 1416, the year in which Poggio Bracciolini discovered the treatises of Vitruvius in the Monastery of San Gallo.

—When did the Greek Revival appear in England? Following the publication of *The Antiquities of Athens*, the Adam brothers began to copy Greek decoration, and when, in 1800, Lord Elgin brought back from Athens his splendid collection of architectural fragments, now in the British Museum, the Greek Revival ran riot.

—What brought about the birth of the Neo-Classic? In the second half of the 18th century, excavations were made at Pompeii and Herculaneum, and these determined the reaction to Rococo. In England, Burlington's book, *Palladio's Antiquities of Rome,* and the work of Chambers helped create a similar phenomenon.

—And the Gothic Revival? In France it was connected with the work of Viollet-le-Duc, in England with the influence of Ruskin who, in the second half of the 19th century, concurred in the decision of Sir Charles Barry and Augustus W. Pugin to reconstruct the Houses of Parliament in Perpendicular Gothic.

The materialist interpretation has infinite aspects, and it is still widely held today. It may be wagered that more than one reader, reflecting on our description of S. Maria in Cosmedin (pl. 9), will have thought: "What strange mental contortions to explain those wall-sec-

Fig. 29. A racial and sociological interpretation of architecture by Irving K. Pond (see Bibliography).

172

F. Borromini: Dome of S. Carlino alle Quattro Fontane, Rome (1638-41).

Plate 13. Movement and interpenetration of Baroque space

173

F. Borromini: Interior of
Sant'Ivo alla Sapienza, Rome
(1642-62).

B. Neumann: Vierzehnheil-
igen (Church of the Fourteen
Saints), Main (1743-72).

Plate 13. Movement and interpenetration of Baroque space

175

F. Borromini: Dome of Sant'-
Ivo alla Sapienza, Rome
(1642-62).

Baldassarre Longhena: S. Maria della Salute, Venice (1631-87).

Plate 13. Movement and interpenetration of Baroque space

176

Pietro da Cortona: Dome of San Carlo al
Corso, Rome (1665).

Pietro da Cortona: Santa Maria della Pace,
Rome (1656).

Plate 13. Movement and interpenetration of Baroque space

177

F. Juvara: Palace of Stupinigi (begun 1729).

Plate 14. Movement and interpenetration of Baroque space

179

G. Guarini: Dome of San
Lorenzo, Turin (1668-87).

F. Juvara: Aerial view of the Palace of Stupinigi.

Plate 14. Movement and interpenetration of Baroque space

180

Le Corbusier and P. Jeanneret: Interior view of the Villa Savoie, Poissy (1928-30). See also pl. 4.

Mies van der Rohe: Pavilion, Barcelona Exposition (1929). Interior views.

Mies van der Rohe: Pavilion, Barcelona Exposition (1929).

Plate 15. The open plan of modern architecture

W. Gropius: Bauhaus, Dessau (1925-26). See also pl. 20.

Plate 15. The open plan of modern architecture

182

Philip C. Johnson: House, New Canaan, Conn. (1949). Exterior and interior.

Plate 15. The open plan of modern architecture

183

Skidmore, Owings and Merrill: Lever House, New York (1952).

tions. There is another, extremely simple reason: in the old church there was a gallery and, because it was too heavy, wall-sections were substituted for some of the columns. That's all there was to it!"

The racial interpretation is adequately described by figure 29.

Naturalistic or imitative interpretations are fairly well known also. According to them, for example, the forms of the Greek column and capital reflect their origin in bundles of branches topped by terracotta bricks, which served to support the architrave of the earliest temples. When one wonders why contemporary Scandinavian architecture does not have the formal austerity of European Functionalism, why Swedish and Finnish architects are more human and organic in their work than a Le Corbusier, some materialists reply that trees in Scandinavia grow along curved lines and thus inspire less block-like architecture than that of reinforced concrete and steel.

Technical Interpretation

Of all positivist interpretations the most prevalent by far is the technical. There is no question that the history of its construction is so important a part of the history of a monument that without it a critical study appears defective, abstract and remote. But technical interpretation has been so abused that it is worth a brief discussion.

The argument that architectonic forms are *determined* by technics of construction is, it seems to me, in error. If anything, history shows the opposite process: forms tend to repeat technics that have actually been superseded. For example, Egyptian forms continued to be modelled according to the branches used in primitive structures, even centuries after stone had been the material in use; the Greek orders took their profiles from wooden elements of the archaic temple and translated them into marble; the rusticated masonry of the High Renaissance was cut into squares independently of the way in which the actual stones were cut; in the 19th century false stonework was drawn on plaster, and walls were given an icing of painted marble and wood; finally, today, instead of exploiting the great possibilities of continuous resistance offered by reinforced concrete and of modelling structures non-geometrically to achieve effects as in Mendelsohn's Einstein Tower, we generally press concrete into columns and beams, repeating the forms of metal construction.

Technocratic concepts and the slogan, "the beauty of the machine," accompanied every avant-garde movement of the first quarter of our century. But functionalists, who went into ecstasies over an automobile and extolled its rationality, failed to ask themselves why the motor was placed in front, despite the problem of transmission to the rear wheels, and did not suspect that this inconvenient arrangement probably was a carry-over from horse-and-buggy days, when the motive power was always out in front, under the eyes of the driver.

The most incredible thing is to find archeologists dedicating their lives to the structural features of monuments who depreciate any critical contribution and exult over the discovery of the slightest technical detail, and who, at the same time, are reactionaries with respect to modern architecture. If the technical interpreters consider architecture an instrument for enlarging the horizon of human life, how can they fail to make the proper comparison between the static, stony equilibrium of old-fashioned building and the splendid mechanism of modern housing with its lighting facilities and central heating, its elevators, bathrooms, washing machines, fire-control systems, incinerators, pneumatic tubes, telephones and television? Certainly if technics were the basis of everything, theoreticians of mechanical functionalism, who wax so enthusiastic over the energy and dynamism of modern architecture, would be completely and always right.

Traditional handbooks of architectural practice, in recognition of this challenge, try to make a distinction between real construction and apparent construction, between practical engineering and esthetic engineering. They have proclaimed that it is not enough for a building actually to be structurally solid; it must also have an appearance of solidity. And what is this apparent solidity? A facing of rough stone three-quarters of an inch thick, which gives the impression that the house is built of stone. Leaving the corners of a building solid or reinforcing them with quoins, when today they can be completely opened up as windows (pls. 16, 17). "Apparent solidity" is not an *a priori* law; it is simply the old solidity, the habit of observing traditional weight relationships. Indeed modernists are right who say that a new feeling for structure must follow new technics.

Palladio's Palazzo Chiericati is as much suspended on columns (pl. 12) as Le Corbusier's Villa at Poissy (pl. 15). If the columns of the earlier building "seem" more solid than those of the later one, and if the columns coupled at the sides of the "solid" would comfort Schopenhauer much more than the *pilotis*, these reactions do not depend on absolute laws of physiological gravitation, but on an inveterate habit of accepting static equilibriums of the past. Falling Water is a case in point. The story goes that when the moment arrived to pull down the last support of the scaffolding form in which the great cantilevered terrace had been cast, the workmen refused to carry out the job. The heads of the builders' union, called to the site, politely informed Mr. Wright that they were not prepared to pay insurance to the families of the two men who would certainly be buried under the debris of that architectural "lunacy." When Wright, enraged, seized an axe and attacked the support by himself, some of the workmen fled. Yet the terrace, as we can see (pl. 16), is still intact after eighteen years.

In conclusion, the functionalist interpretation, in its two-fold significance of utilitarianism and technicalism, is the result of a mental inhibition. Born in revolt against the "art for art's sake" standard of the traditionalists, who, ironically, had no art, born with apologies for the modern industrial world and the immanent and social ends of architecture, this inhibition has resulted in a fixation on the second part of the formula, *art and technics*, which has been used arbitrarily from the beginning to divide architectural production into two false parts.

Physio-Psychological Interpretations

It will not be worth the trouble to linger over those psychological interpretations that are generic literary evocations of "states of the soul" produced by architectural "styles." The equations are familiar: the

Egyptian = age of fear, when man was dedicated to the preservation of a body without which he would not be able to achieve reincarnation; the Greek = age of grace, symbol of a contemplative truce in the riot of passions; the Roman = age of force and pompousness; the Early Christian = age of piety and love; the Gothic = age of aspiration; the Renaissance = age of elegance; the Revivals = age of memory.

On another level entirely, and fundamental to any history of architectural interpretations, is the theory of *Einfuehlung* or empathy. According to this theory, esthetic emotion consists in the spectator's identifying himself with the forms viewed and correspondingly in the fact that architecture transcribes states of feeling into structural forms, humanizing and animating them. Looking at architectural features, we "vibrate" in affinity with them, since they arouse reactions both in our bodies and in our minds. With these considerations as its premise, symbolistic *Einfuehlung* attempts to reduce art to a science: a building becomes nothing but a machine for producing certain predetermined human reactions. The casuistry it applies to geometrical elements goes as follows:

The horizontal line (pls. 5, 11, 15, 20). When "following a horizontal line in instinctive mimicry, man feels a sense of the immanent, the rational, the intellectual. It is parallel to the earth on which man walks and accordingly accompanies his movement; it extends itself at eye level and thus creates no illusions about its length; in following its path man generally meets some obstacle which emphasizes its limits.

The vertical line (pls. 10, 17). Symbol of the infinite, of ecstasy, of emotion. To follow it, man must halt and raise his eyes to heaven, leaving, for a time, his normal visual direction. The vertical line loses itself in the sky, never meets obstacles or limits, is deceptive about its length, and is thus a symbol of the sublime. Some authors distinguish, in features like volutes, between the ascending line, which represents joy, and the descending, which causes sadness.

Straight lines and curved lines (pls. 3, 20). Straight lines signify resoluteness, rigidity, strength. Curved lines represent hesitancy, flexibility, decorative values.

The spiral (pl. 13) is the symbol of ascension, detachment, of being freed from earthly matters.

The cube (pl. 18) represents integrity, because its dimensions are all equal and immediately comprehensible, and so gives the observer a feeling of certainty.

The circle (pls. 6, 11) gives a sense of equilibrium, of mastery, of control over the whole of life.

The sphere, and thus the hemispherical dome (pls. 8, 12, 17, 19), represents perfection, the final conclusive law.

The ellipse (pl. 13), having two centers, never permits the eye to rest, keeps it moving and unquiet.

The interpenetration of geometric forms is the symbol of dynamism and continuous movement.

These are examples of the semantics of *Einfuehlung* which analyzes "scientifically" the extension of the *ego*, both on the part of the architect and the observer, in architectural elements. The grammar is provided by proportion, rhythm, symmetry, eurhythmy, contrast and all the other qualities of architecture which we shall analyze in their place under the formalistic interpretation and to which *Einfuehlung* offers a physio-psychological substratum.

It is always easy to go from a *science* of the beautiful to a *rule* of the beautiful. The philosophy of empathy has given new prestige to three earlier interpretations of architecture: *a) the interpretation of proportions,* which holds that just as there is a musical scale congenitally attuned to human physiology, so there are architectonic proportions which are beautiful *per se.* Some writers have even attempted to translate architectonic proportions into music (fig. 30); *b) the geometric-mathematical interpretation,* which provoked the rhetorical eloquence of Viollet-le-Duc, Thiersche, Zeising and Ghyka. More judicious writers limit themselves to pointing out the geometrics latent in many architectural compositions (fig. 31), but others, in the name of "spatial, cosmic and nuclear harmonies," abandon themselves to long dissertations on Egyptian triangles, the Golden Section, on combinations of Euclidean harmonies, analogical modules, the most abstruse interpolations and on dynamic symmetry; *c) the anthropomorphic interpretation,*

189

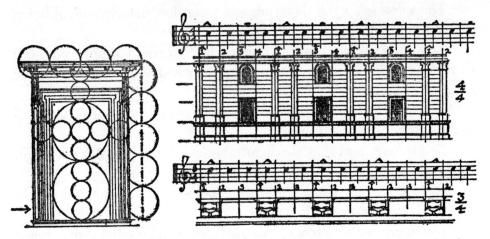

Fig. 30. A musical interpretation of architecture by Claude Bragdon. *Left*: The door of S. Lorenzo in Damasco, Rome, translated into octaves, fifths and thirds. *Right:* The top story of Palazzo Giraud, Rome, translated into 4/4, and the cornice of Palazzo della Farnesina, Rome, translated into 3/4.

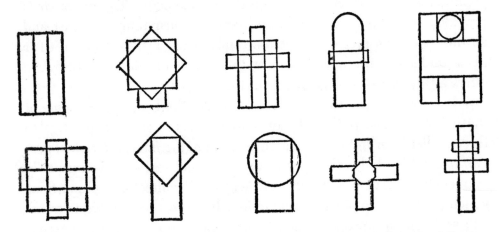

Fig. 31. Claude Bragdon's interpretation of the "latent geometrics" in the following structures: 1st line, L. to R.: Temple of Zeus, Agrigento; Michelangelo's plan for St. Peter's; Certosa, Pavia; Notre Dame, Paris; Whitehall by Jones; 2nd line: St. Peter's by Bramante; Cathedral of Florence; Pantheon; Church of S. Simeone; Cathedral of Salisbury.

initiated by Vitruvius, who, in homage to the Aristotelian theory of mimesis or imitation, justified the orders of classical architecture by their consonance with the human body. Even today a number of critics continue to toil along this road (fig. 32).

Fig. 32. Anthropomorphic interpretation of architecture. *Left:* Origin of Doric and Ionic capitals according to Pond. *Right:* Origin of the Campanile by Giotto, Florence, and of the Doric column according to Bragdon.

Proceeding from its grammar to its expression, the theory of *Einfuehlung* covers an entire building. For its advocates, all architectural criticism consists in the ability to transfer our very spirit into a building, humanizing it, making it talk, vibrating with it in an unconscious symbiosis in which our body tends to repeat the movement of the architecture. Undoubtedly this theory has the great merit of having thawed the cold abstractness of the critic's dictionary of architecture and of having created a familiarity, a sense of interchange, a human relationship between architecture and man.

A line can be bold or feeble, taut or slack, powerful or fluid. A surface can be trite, crowded with eclectic elements or broad and serene like that of Palazzo Farnese (pl. 2), congested like that of Michelangelo's entrance to the Laurentian Library (pl. 12), insipid and mute like that of Sacconi's Monument to Victor Emmanuel II (pl. 1), strong and dramatic, as in the apse of the Cathedral of Monreale (pl. 18). For the volumes, the important thing is the sense of weight, of pressure and resistance, and these can be massive as in the Baths of Caracalla (pl. 17); articulated and solidly placed, as in the Bauhaus (pl. 20); flexible and politely inviting, as in the Johnson Building (pl. 3); frantically tense, as in the skyscrapers of New York (pl. 17); sweet, exquisitely feminine, almost redolent of the boudoir, as in the Taj Mahal (pl. 17); powerful and austere, as in St. Peter's (pl. 19); gladsome and varied, as

191

in the English farmhouse (pl. 20); elegant and suggestive of the drawing-room, as in the Barcelona Pavilion of Mies van der Rohe (pl. 15); cheerful or awesome, flouting the sense of human instability, as in Wright's Falling Water (pl. 16).

Old esthetic theories maintained that of all the arts, architecture offered the most restricted scale of emotions. It represented calm (Greek), strength (Roman), or ecstasy (Gothic). The theory of empathy broke down this preconception and attributed all the expressions of man to architecture, including a sense of the farcical and the comic in mannered and affected buildings, a sense of the nauseating in vulgar, rhetorical and falsely monumental buildings. It also used to be said that architecture's expression is not descriptive, but static. *Einfuehlung,* through the method of identifying man with form, has demonstrated the contrary; far from being static, architecture moves continually under the continuous rotation of the sun.

"Although there are poems of love, stories of love, paintings of love, and music of love, an architecture of love is inconceivable," Talbot Hamlin states. But compare the Taj Mahal with the Philadelphia Life Insurance Building and then say whether it does not represent love, at least to the extent that one piece of music, with respect to another, may be defined as love music.

Criticism based on empathy has been extended even to the floor-plan of a building. As we say, a tower "rises," a spire "ascends," a circular stair "winds," so it can be said that the atrium of the Pantheon "expands" into the great circular space at the center (fig. 17), or that the living room of Falling Water "grows" or "stretches" into the suspended terrace (fig. 28).

From physio-psychological criticism and its deductions it is a short step to the psychoanalytical interpretation. Alluded to by Claude Bragdon in his theory of duality and trinity (fig. 33), it has not yet been as thoroughly explored in the field of architecture as in painting and literature. Scattered observations are common, however; an early example is Sir Christopher Wren's explanation that man's delight in columns is a prenatal disposition inherited from our ancestors who prayed in groves of trees and worshipped pillars as gods. In addition, the widespread

192

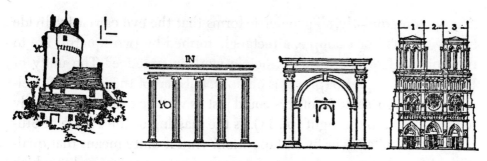

Fig. 33. Bragdon's theory of duality and trinity in architecture. YO denotes the masculine, IN the feminine (see Bibliography).

antipathy for subway tunnels and underground passages is explained in the light of modern neuroses. Lucian Blaga, the Romanian philosopher, in discussing the concept of the "feeling for space" in Riegl, Frobenius and Spengler, discerns in it a phenomenon of the unconscious and seeks the relations between the concept of "sensed" space and the psychology of unfathomable voids. All this, however, remains in the sphere of esthetics and not in the field of architectural criticism.

Formalist Interpretation

Traditional esthetics lists a tiresome series of *laws*, *qualities*, *rules* and *principles* to which architectural composition must correspond, such as unity, contrast, symmetry, balance, proportion, character, scale, style, truth, expression, urbanity, emphasis or accentuation, variety, sincerity, propriety. As we can see, we are asked to consider at the same time both formal qualities, and moral and psychological qualities. Let us analyze them:

Unity. The aim of every artist is to express a single idea in his work. Every composition, both in plan and elevation, must be characterized by a connection between all its components. Composition is the opposite of juxtaposition, where the strength of connected speech is lacking and there is only a series of disjointed words without meaning. Two equivalent and adjacent statues, two identical houses, two stories of the same height, one above the other, do not form a unity, but a

193

duality; consequently, all geometric forms that the eye can easily divide into two parts (for example, a rectangle formed by two squares) are to be avoided. How does this principle work in practice? The unity of Bramante's Tempietto (pl. 12) is obvious, but that of the Palazzo Rucellai much less so, since its orders could just as well be extended endlessly to the left and to the right (pl. 11). Is the massing of the Palace of Stupinigi done unitarily or by juxtaposition? And if unity means that quality which makes every element of a work of art necessary and to which nothing can be added or subtracted, would the unity of the Philadelphia Life Insurance Building be destroyed if it were raised another two stories?

Symmetry. This is the balance of formal, axial buildings. Symmetrical constructions include the Arch of Titus and the Victor Emmanuel Monument (pl. 1), Palazzo Farnese (pl. 2), the Parthenon (pl. 5), S. Sabina (pl. 7), S. Ambrogio (pl. 9), Palazzo Strozzi and S. Spirito (pl. 11), Palazzo Chiericati (pl. 12), the Taj Mahal and the Galerie des Machines in Paris (pl. 17), the Cathedral of Monreale and La Rotonda (pl. 18), the Schocken Store (pl. 19) and Borromini's courtyard (pl. 20). Examples of asymmetrical buildings include Falling Water (pls. 2 and 16), the Johnson Building (pl. 3), the Palazzo Vecchio in Florence (pl. 11), Mies van der Rohe's Barcelona Pavilion (pl. 15), the living room of Taliesin (pl. 19), the farmhouse at Whitemarsh, the Shuckle Office Building and the Bauhaus (pl. 20). To correspond to the canon of unity, however, these asymmetrical buildings must obey the law of equilibrium or balance.

Balance. This is the symmetry of informal, non-axial architecture. According to this rule, a plane placed in the central part of a building, even though it cannot be seen, calls for masses of the same "weight" on both sides. In the simplest terms, if we place an equal number of metal weights on either side of a pair of scales, the result will be equilibrium; if the weights are arranged in the same way on both sides of the scales, we have symmetry; if they are heaped up on one side and placed in a row on the other, we have balance. The Torre del Mangia in Siena has the same "weight" as the palace that extends horizontally to its right; the wing that comes forward to the left in the Barcelona Pavilion

194

(pl. 15) has the same weight of gravity as the smooth wall extending to the right; the second-story terrace of Falling Water (pl. 16 and fig. 28) is not centered with respect to that of the first story, but the open canopy and the vertical line of the chimney balance its mass. If this were not so, the psychologists maintain, we should feel physically troubled, as if something were missing, as if we were listing to one side, as if we had an arm amputated; in other words, the want of balance in a building would cause, by symbolic sympathy, a feeling of amputation in our own bodies.

Emphasis or accentuation.   In every composition it is necessary to have a center of visual interest, a focal point for the eye. This may be the apex in the Pyramid of Caius Cestus (pl. 1); the portal in Palazzo Farnese (pl. 2); the center of the pediment in the Parthenon (pl. 5); the apse in Early Christian and Byzantine churches (pls. 7 and 8); the dome of Hagia Sophia, the Pazzi Chapel, St. Peter's and S. Lorenzo (pls. 8, 11, 19, 14); the convex central section of Stupinigi (pl. 14); the chimney-shafts in the farmhouse at Whitemarsh (pl. 20); or the interlacing of linear roses in the Wladislavski Hall in Prague (pl. 20). Are there exceptions? The Colosseum is one, with its unaccented, uniform curved mass. So is the Philadelphia Life Insurance Building (pl. 17), for no center of interest can be singled out in it. However, all the other works illustrated obey, more or less strictly, this rule of emphasis.

Contrast.   Unity is to be understood as a synthesis of contrasting elements, not as a static, inert uniformity of parts. For a building to be *alive*, it must show contrast between vertical and horizontal lines, between solids and voids, between defined and intangible forms, between volumes and between masses. And for full expression, the dominance of one element or the other, or of a third, is needed. In the Arch of Titus (pl. 1) neither the horizontals nor the verticals prevail; it is the arch that is dominant. Neither the verticals, the horizontals nor any other kind of element has mastery in the Victor Emmanuel Monument (pl. 1), and that is a primary reason why it is an inert, lifeless pile. If Michelangelo had not added his heavy cornice to Palazzo Farnese, it might have been as lifeless, since the horizontals scarcely prevail over the verticals and the solids balance the voids. It is evident that verticals prevail in Gothic

195

churches (pl. 10), that solids dominate in Palazzo Vecchio (pl. 11), and that the opposite is true in Palazzo Chiericati (pl. 12). The horizontal prevails in Falling Water (pl. 16), but if the vertical elements were not there, and thus there were no contrast, the whole composition would appear to sag to the ground. As it stands, it is vibrantly alive even in the contrasts in texture of the materials, now smooth, now rough, and in the contrasts of color.

Proportion. The most common definition is this: the relation of the parts to each other and to the whole of the building. But no matter how it is defined, proportion is the means by which a building is divided to achieve the qualities of unity, balance, emphasis, contrast, as well as harmony and rhythm. But we have already had occasion to observe the absurdity of a mechanistic thesis of proportion, whether in the geometric, mathematical or musical sense, since proportion is closely tied to the scale of a building.

Scale. Illustrating the scale of a building is exactly the opposite of what we have done in the plates accompanying our text, where the dimensions of the photographs have been established without relationship to actual dimensions, and where often we have preferred to illustrate a detail in greater size than the illustration of an entire building. This would have been a mistake in a systematic history of architecture, in which all buildings should be drawn to the same scale and each should have indicated close to it the height of the average man. If the Temple of Karnak in Egypt were as tall as the Parthenon, we should have a composition not too dissimilar to the Greek temple: vertical elements supporting the architrave. The Egyptian temple, however, is tremendously higher (fig. 34), a man cannot see the architrave above the columns, and consequently the expression at Karnak is entirely different from that of Hellenic balance. Scale is therefore an essential element in judging architecture. One thing should be kept clear, however: if man is the measure of all things, if it is an error to establish proportion without establishing scale, it is also a mistake to establish scale without proportion. One building may be huge in dimensional scale, like the interior of St. Peter's, and another may be small in scale, like Borromini's S. Carlino; yet the second may appear much more spacious

Fig. 34. The principle of scale in architecture. *Left:* Sections of the Egyptian temples of Philae and Edfu (by Pond). *Right:* Illustration of Trystan Edward's principle of human scale and monumental-commercial scale (see Bibliography).

than the first. Generally, a tall building stands out in a city, but the scale is inverted in New York (pl. 17), where, in the mass of skyscrapers in the Wall Street area, the little Trinity Church dominates its surroundings precisely because of its smallness. The principle of scale is thus not to be confused with the anthropomorphic interpretation we mentioned in the preceding chapter. Scale means dimension with respect to man's visual apprehension, dimension with respect to man's physical size. A building wholly of monumental scale, as in so many examples of the Fascist pseudo-modern style, is empty and silly; but the monumental scale of Hagia Sophia (pl. 8), of Amiens (pl. 10), of S. Ivo (pl. 13), continually related to elements on a human scale, is magnificently effective. In dialectic sensitivity to architectural scale the Baroque was pre-eminent. In the last hundred years, however, enormous crimes have been perpetrated against it, for example, the destruction of Regent Street in London at the hands of Norman Shaw, and the ruination of St. Peter's Square in Rome by the demolition of the Spina dei Borghi, of which nothing remains but a nostalgic photograph (pl. 19).

Expression or character. Everyone agrees that architecture must have an expressive function, but difficulties arise when we ask what it must express. If it is the feeling and personality of the architect, the problem concerns esthetics. If it is to be psychological expression, the objection, as we suggested in the preceding paragraph, is that even a dummy can have unity, symmetry or balance, emphasis, contrast, pro-

197

portion and scale; but if it has no life, expression or physiognomy, if it has nothing to say, it will never be a living creation. The character of nobility, practicality, refinement, humor, urbanity, vulgarity, dignity, ostentation, smiling strength, as in the Church of the Salute in Venice, of oppressiveness, as in Michelangelo, is to be found in architectural, as in human, expression. Familiarizing ourselves with the various languages, numerous dialects, infinite physiognomical variations of building, is a question of sensitivity. In the case of a building, as with a man, it is a question of being able sensitively to read not only its static expression—calm or agitated, business-like or social, generous or mean, modest or vainglorious and affected—that is, its temperament, but also its dynamic character, its crescendos, its passages from pianissimo to fortissimo, the tone of its state of mind besides the tone of its being. To superficial observers there are no neurotics among the Chinese, who are judged to be polite, self-controlled, ceremonious, as apparently there is no neurosis in the community of Greek temples; but it is a question of sensitivity and familiarity to be able to recognize the inhibited manifestation of hysterics in China or of agitation in the Greek temple. And if Borromini appears violent and excited, while Giuliano da Maiano seems dignified and restrained, it is a question of sensitivity to perceive how much of their manner is simply stylistic education and how much is personal expression; in other words, when is it that Borromini, always gesticulating, is actually calm and collected; and when is it that Giuliano da Maiano, always well-dressed, smiling and composed, is in his own heart, or in the heart of one of his buildings, frenzied and furious? If this psychological, not formal, quality of expression is taken into account, there will be no difficulty in disposing of all the moralistic preconceptions that have grown out of it. If it is said, "A building should express exactly what it is and what its aim is supposed to be," the reply should be, "Neither more nor less than a man must express what he is and what the object of his life might be." Anyone who holds that men should go around naked, so as not to clothe their reality, and should have their names, temperaments, principal interests, professions and so forth written on their foreheads, may claim that buildings should do likewise. Here, too, it is a question of common sense. We do not like men who pretend to be something they are not, and so we do not like buildings that wear a false face, whether it be pseudo-monumental or pseudo-functionalist. A single great glass front which conceals the division between the floors of a building, or, correspondingly, a large hall indicated on the exterior as two floors, is a deception; and a deception, if it is not to be pitied, is certainly not to be recommended.

Truth. Should buildings be true or false? Should they be sincere? There is no need to assume the air of a Puritan Grand Inquisitor, as Ruskin did, to elicit an affirmative reply. If the Pyramid of Caius Cestus (pl. 1) were pointed out to you with the words, "There is the smartest night club in Rome," you would be taken aback. If you were told, "The Palazzo Chiericati is a low-cost dwelling, designed for rapid construction," you would be right to protest against the falseness, the insincerity of an architect incapable of conceiving a building except in terms of courtly pomp. If you were shown Mendelsohn's Schocken Store with the comment, "Look at that beautiful church!" you would be amazed, since the effect is entirely that of a multi-story commercial building. Take care, however, for on this terrain of "honest expression" it is very easy to slip into associative and symbolic confusion. You may be told, "The expression of a prison should be one of steep, stony, rusticated walls, which give the impression that escape would not be easy," or, "The windows of a bank should be as few in number and as small as possible to give a sense of security, of being burglar-proof," or, still worse, "A church should be Gothic, because that is the religious style," or, "A palace should be Baroque, because only the Baroque can give one a sense of luxury and grandeur." With this kind of thinking, we are led away from the realities of architecture into an empty sphere of anachronistic, archeological and literary associations, where the habits of conformism prevail. This is not all; it should also be noted that honesty and truth in architecture, as in life, should be controlled by propriety.

Propriety. According to the fanatics of "honest construction," if a floor is built of beams, it is dishonest not to leave them exposed; but the property of a floor is to be able to walk on it, and this property is worth much more than structural "honesty." As among men, so among buildings, there are liars by profession, and they are odious. There are also those who must always speak the truth, unburden themselves, tell all, describe their personal history in the most intimate details, even when no one wants to hear them—and they are no less irritating.

Urbanity. This is the quality that is lacking in "monumental" architects, egocentrics, publicity-seekers; in those who want to impose their personalities; in men as in buildings (fig. 34). We who live at a time when every artist believes he has a message of universal importance to give the world; when everyone is intent on being original, on inventing something new, on standing out in social competition, on being pre-eminent; when everyone believes he is cleverer than others— we are surrounded by buildings that may have all the qualities, but certainly not that of urbanity. If you observe in the new sections of our cities the stridency of the colors and marbles, of the shapes of the balconies and the heights of the cornices, you will see how these attempts at originality result, in their ensemble, in a monotony greater by far than that of some urban sections built in the 18th and even in the 19th century, in which a civil way of life reigned among the buildings. Modern speculative construction gives the effect of a cocktail party where everyone, whether intelligent or stupid, wants to be the life of the party, cut a fine figure, speak, shout, attract the attention of his neighbor, while no one listens to anyone else. The result is an impenetrable din that makes you think nostalgically of the polite, slightly inhibited, instructive and pleasant conversation of the people, as of the buildings, of past centuries. The discerning eye discovers true values even when they are not apparent; and he who is in a hurry to be noticed often has little to say.

Style. This is the language, or rather the linguistics, of design. And when our pedantic, traditionalist pedant asks, "Is it forbidden to build a house in an ancient style?" he can be answered with another question, "Is it possible today spontaneously to write a poem in Latin?" Whoever has anything to say, expresses it simply, in the language current. He who has nothing to say, may hope to deceive us by hiding, under an elegant garb of erudition, his inner emptiness. Just as language is not static or immutable, so styles change; and that is why, as

200

F. Ll. Wright: Falling Water, Bear Run, Penna. (1936).

Plate 16. Organic space of modern architecture

201

F. Ll. Wright: Falling Water, Bear Run, Penna. (1936).

202

Plate 16. Organic space of modern architecture

F. Ll. Wright: Unitarian Church, Madison, Wis. (1951).

F. Ll. Wright: Falling Water,
Bear Run, Penna. (1936).

F. Ll. Wright: Friedman House, Pleasantville, N. Y. (1949).

Plate 16. Organic space of modern architecture

204

New York: Skyscrapers.

Taj Mahal, Agra, India (1630).

New York: Seen from the west of Manhattan
toward Rockefeller Center (1932-40).

G. Howe and W. Lescaze: Philadelphia Life
Insurance Building (1932).

Galerie des Machines, Paris Exhibition, 1889.

Plate 17. Across the history of architecture

205

Aerial view of Venetian houses (15th century).

Plate 17. Across the history of architecture

Plate 17. Across the history of architecture

Baths of Caracalla, Rome (211-217 A.D.).

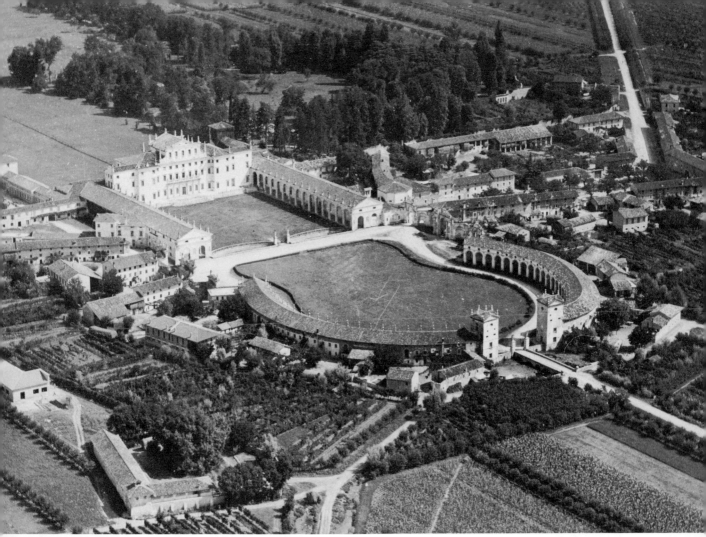

Villa Manin, Passariano (17th-18th century).

Plate 17. Across the history of architecture

A. Palladio: Villa Capra, called La Rotonda, near Vicenza (begun 1550).

Plate 18. Across the history of architecture.

Domes of S. Giovanni degli Eremiti, Palermo (ca. 1132).

209

Cathedral of Monreale. Apse (1166-89).

Plate 18. Across the history of architecture

Cathedral of Trani (12th century). Interior.

Charles Eames: House, Santa Monica, Cal.
(1949). Interior.

Nourago at Isili, Sardinia. Interior.

Charles Eames: House, Santa Monica, Cal.
(1949). Exterior.

Trulli, Alberobello.

Plate 18. Across the history of architecture

211

Aerial view of the excavations at Pompei.

Plate 18. Across the history of architecture

212

has by now been recognized in our culture, tracing the history of "styles" has no meaning if one grants that each person, and especially each artist, employs language for individual meaning and expression, and so creates his own language. But as it is true that producing modern architecture, in other words, using contemporary language, does not necessarily mean creating art; so it is unquestionable that employing extraneous academic language means precluding any possibility of speaking spontaneously, and so of creating poetry.

❀   ❀   ❀   ❀

The foregoing are the chief qualities or principles of architecture as they are enumerated in traditional esthetics. For those who are interested, as many more may be found in the bibliography at the end of this book. We have not gone into the "principles" of livability, design, eurhythmy, harmony, consonance or rhythm, because we believe they are either implicit in the qualities we have discussed or are common to all the arts.

We are dealing, it will be apparent, with moralistic, psychological and formalistic principles. The great contribution of contemporary art criticism has consisted in the coming to maturity of *formalistic* criticism. To pass from vague concepts of symmetry, contrast, variety, emphasis (trouble brews when they are made specific, for rules and dogmas of composition are then laid down) to modern architectural criticism is like going from the simple categories of a critic like Mengs—chiaroscuro, coloring, harmony, grace—to the penetrating schemas of a Fiedler and a Wölfflin. The wonder is to observe how these schemas of contemporary art criticism, of which no historian of painting and sculpture is allowed ignorance, are still so little applied in architectural criticism. Yet it is clear that Wölfflin's five symbols of pure visibility—on the one hand, the *linear*, the *vision of the surface*, the *closed form, multiplicity, absolute clearness;* on the other, the *pictorial*, the *vision of depth, open form, unity* and *relative clearness*—have a most evident application to architecture, all the more as they were born of the critical rehabilitation of Baroque architecture. Who can fail to see the plastic definiteness, the tactile values, of Bramante's Tempietto (pl. 12), the vision of depth in S. Ivo alla Sapienza (pl. 13), the closed form of the Parthenon (pl. 5) compared to the open form of Neumann's Vierzehn-heilungen (pl. 13), the multiplicity of the coordinated and juxtaposed parts of Palladio's Rotonda (pl. 18) and the unity of Mies van der Rohe's Pavilion?

In an effort toward more exact individuation, more acute determination and more fitting comparison between single works of art, modern criticism in architecture, as in other figurative arts, has multiplied the symbols of pure visibility. Leaving aside whatever dangers it may run of falling into occultism, it surely has the great merit of having formulated a fuller and more accurate vocabulary of criteria than "the balance of solids and voids," "the play of mass" and "volumetric relationships." Today we can speak of non-limited space and of perspective space, of pictorial qualification of surfaces, of spatial infinity and of chromatic values, of atmospheric depth, of linear interweaving against a void, and of continually varying relationships between color planes and chiaroscuro-depths, between wall masses and masses resolved in surfaces. This effort toward critical precision means searching for the individual life of each monument, separating it from the common denominator of its "style" and promoting a finer response to its esthetic value.

On the Spatial Interpretation

This summary of the interpretations of architecture shows that they can be divided into three major categories, as we indicated earlier in this chapter:

a) interpretations according to content;
b) physio-psychological interpretations;
c) formalistic interpretations.

All historians adopt one of these three interpretations as their principal method, but each adds some observations that derive from the other two methods. It is difficult to find a history of architecture that deals entirely with content or one that is exclusively formalistic.

214

The doctrine of the *purely visual* still has an important function in the history of architecture, which for centuries has been pervaded by a positivist mentality. It is obvious, however, that its deficiencies, which have already been pointed out by the best critics in the field of painting, would also be evident in its full application to architecture. Lines, surfaces, light and shade, mass and pictorial values, atmospheric depths, solids and voids, and all the most subtle of visual symbols—despite their great usefulness as preliminary education in freeing criticism of traditional preconceptions—do not suffice to explain the profound difference between one work of art and another, and are therefore inadequate for the critical individuation of architects or buildings. They give rise to much less all-inclusive, thus much more useful, categories than the traditional antitheses of *classic* and *romantic, formal* and *picturesque,* but they give us neither the history, nor, as a consequence, the reality, of a work of art.

The drawbacks of formalistic criticism are revealed clearly in architecture. In painting, as a matter of fact, it is relatively easy for a critic to apply formalistic standards broadly, and then, when he realizes he has stated very similar notions about two works that may really be quite far apart, to distinguish between them by drawing attention to their different content. Art criticism is still engaged in the *content vs. form* debate, which in literary criticism has been resolved in a dialectic accord; but while it is easy for formalists to characterize a painting by helpful references to its subject matter almost without our notice, when we turn to architecture—an entirely abstract art, as it is said, without representational values—the need for characterization becomes even more obvious.

Let us consider the problem of *content* in architecture. If you examine the photographs illustrating this book, you will notice a strange fact: with the exception of the Monument to Victor Emmanuel II (pl. 1), Hagia Sophia (pl. 8) and the fortuitous case of some snapshots taken of the interior of the Johnson Building (pl. 4), almost none of the photographs includes a human figure. The houses, churches and even the squares are deserted, abandoned, unfleshed specters—"abstractions," if you like. The Wladislavski Hall (pl. 20) is a glacial play of lines and pictorial surfaces without content. The Temple of Minerva Medica (pl. 6) has a touch of humanity, perhaps because the photographer was tired of repeating, "one side, please," to the passersby or found it too much trouble to move the cart we see on the left. But Westminster, Amiens and King's College Chapel (pl. 10) appear to be little more than dead-looking mineral formations left standing after the destruction of the human race, for whom, however, those spaces and chairs were obviously intended.

There is no cause for wonder that, as in painting, tactile values have been sought, so in architecture anthropomorphic and physio-psychological theories have been developed in a desperate attempt to give form a human content. Since the beauty of a building had been considered completely independent of its social value, the question inevitably arose: "For *whom* is it beautiful?" The answer had to be, "For man." "And why is it beautiful for him?" "Because it arouses innate harmonies like those of the musical scales"; or, "Because it elicits sympathetic reactions in his body." But all this refers to the volumes, the wall-masses, the decoration. What about the *space*?

Here it is worth quoting, at considerable length, Geoffrey Scott, the distinguished English critic, who, although sharing physio-psychological concepts as a student of Berenson, reveals towards the end of his *The Architecture of Humanism* his perception that to speak of lines, surfaces, volumes and masses certainly may have value, but not the specific value of architecture:

"But besides spaces which have merely length and breadth—surfaces, that is to say, at which we look—architecture gives us spaces of three dimensions in which we stand. And here is the very centre of architectural art. The functions of the arts, at many points, overlap; architecture has much that it holds in common with sculpture, and more that it shares with music. But it has also its peculiar province and a pleasure which is typically its own. It has the monopoly of space. Architecture alone of the Arts can give space its full value. It can surround us with a void of three dimensions; and whatever delight may be derived from that is the gift of architecture alone. Painting can

216

depict space; poetry, like Shelley's, can recall its image; music can give us its analogy; but architecture deals with space directly; it uses space as a material and sets us in the midst.

"Criticism has singularly failed to recognize this supremacy in architecture of spatial values. The tradition of criticism is practical. The habits of our mind are fixed on matter. We talk of what occupies our tools and arrests our eyes. Matter is fashioned; space comes. Space is 'nothing'—a mere negation of the solid. And thus we come to overlook it.

"But though we may overlook it, space affects us and can control our spirit; and a large part of the pleasure we obtain from architecture —pleasure which seems unaccountable, or for which we do not trouble to account—springs in reality from space. Even from a utilitarian point of view, space is logically our end. To enclose a space is the object of building; when we build we do but detach a convenient quantity of space, seclude it and protect it, and all architecture springs from that necessity. But aesthetically space is even more supreme. The architect models in space as a sculptor in clay. He designs his space as a work of art; that is, he attempts through its means to excite a certain mood in those who enter it.

"What is his method? Once again his appeal is to Movement. Space, in fact, is liberty of movement. That is its value to us, and as such it enters our physical consciousness. We adapt ourselves instinctively to the spaces in which we stand, project ourselves into them, fill them ideally with our movements. Let us take the simplest of instances. When we enter the end of a nave and find ourselves in a long vista of columns, we begin, almost under compulsion, to walk forward: the character of the space demands it. Even if we stand still, the eye is drawn down the perspective, and we, in imagination, follow it. The space has suggested a movement. Once this suggestion has been set up, everything which accords with it will seem to assist us; everything which thwarts it will appear impertinent and ugly. We shall, moreover, require something to close and satisfy the movement—a window, for example, or an altar; and a blank wall, which would be inoffensive as the termination of an emphasised axis, simply because movement without motive and without climax contradicts our physical instincts: it is not humanised.

"A symmetrical space, on the other hand, duly proportioned to the body—(for not all symmetrical spaces will be beautiful)—invites no movement in any one direction more than another. This gives us equipoise and control; our consciousness returns constantly to the centre, and again is drawn from the centre equally in all directions. But we possess in ourselves a physical memory of just the movement. For we make it every time we draw breath. Spaces of such a character, therefore, obtain an additional entry to our sense of beauty through this elementary sensation of expansion. Unconscious though the process of breathing habitually is, its vital value is so emphatic that any restriction of the normal function is accompanied by pain, and—beyond a certain point—by a peculiar horror; and the slightest assistance to it—as, for example, is noticed in high air—by delight. The need to expand, felt in all our bodily movements, and most crucially in breathing, is not only profound in every individual, but obviously of infinite antiquity in the race. It is not surprising, then, that it should have become the body's veritable symbol of well-being, and that spaces which satisfy it should appear beautiful, those which offend it ugly.

"We cannot, however, lay down fixed proportions of space as architecturally right. Space value in architecture is affected first and foremost, no doubt, by actual dimensions; but it is affected by a hundred considerations besides. It is affected by lighting and the position of shadows: the source of light attracts the eye and sets up an independent suggested movement of its own. It is affected by colour: a dark floor and a light roof give a totally different space sensation to that created by a dark roof and a light floor. It is affected by our own expectancy: by the space we have immediately left. It is affected by the character of the predominating lines: an emphasis on verticals, as is well known, gives an illusion of greater height; an emphasis on horizontals gives a sense of greater breadth. It is affected by projections—both in elevation and in plan—which may cut the space and cause us to feel it, not as one, but several. Thus, in a symmetrical domed church it will depend on the relation of the depth of the transepts to their own width, and to that of

218

the span of the dome, whether we experience it as one space or as five; and a boldly projecting cornice may set the upward limit of space-sensation instead of the actually enclosing roof.

"Nothing, therefore, will serve the architect but the fullest power to imagine the space-value resulting from the complex conditions of each particular case; there are no liberties which he may not sometimes take, and no 'fixed ratios' which may not fail him. Architecture is not a machinery but an art; and those theories of architecture which provide ready-made tests for the creation or criticism of design are self-condemned. None the less, in the beauty of every building, space-value, addressing itself to our sense of movement, will play a principal part." (Geoffrey Scott, *The Architecture of Humanism*, Charles Scribner's Sons, N. Y., 1925; Doubleday Anchor Books, N. Y., 1954, pp. 168-171.)

These pages are incidental in Scott's book, which is dedicated to other problems and, even in the field of "humanist values," is much more concerned with design and plastics, whose possibilities have already been investigated by art criticism. It is an important passage, however, because it expresses, perhaps with greater clarity than other writers have shown in the past, an insight into architectural reality. Any number of historians have indicated, by one allusion or another, that they have grasped, if only for a moment, the secret of architecture; but in this one parenthesis of Scott's discourse intuition has achieved absolute clarity.

Of course, as an advocate of a physio-psychological interpretation, he had at once to translate spatial values into physical appeals. He was thus implicitly and against his will compelled to establish canons. To him, for instance, if the perspective space created by the colonnades of a basilica must terminate in a window or an apse and not in a smooth wall, the Gothic cathedrals, whose horizontal directing lines of movement culminate in large glassed openings, must also be beautiful; the Christian basilicas from S. Sabina (pl. 7) to S. Maria in Cosmedin (pl. 9) must be acceptable. But, according to this reasoning, S. Spirito (pl. 11 and fig. 22) must be pronounced ugly, because it ends in a smooth wall centering on a column—otherwise, what impulse of physical movement is aroused by Brunelleschi's spatial prosody applied to the longitudinal church plan? Another observation: if the physical movement and the movement portrayed coincide, what difference remains between pictorial space and architectural space, which Scott sets in almost mutual opposition at the beginning of the pages cited?

These hazy points do not, however, diminish the value of Scott's fundamental conclusions: 1) that the original, intrinsic value of architecture depends on internal space; 2) that all other factors—volumetric, plastic and decorative elements—count in the judgment of a building according to how well they accentuate, coincide or interfere with the spatial value; 3) that spatial value is concerned with the same elements that are involved in utilitarian value, that is, the elements of the voids themselves.

We have fully discussed the first two conclusions. It is clear, however, that if architectural criticism finally succeeds in translating all the theory and methods of *Einfuehlung* and the purely visual into spatial reality, it will have made great progress and attained the same maturity as plastic criticism, but of necessity it will have been confronted by the same obstacles of "non-individuation." Symmetrical space has an infinite number of ways of expressing itself, but in analyzing works of symmetrical space we should probably say very similar things about different buildings; the individual physiognomy of each building would not be fully established. Again, we should have to look to literary criticism, which has gone beyond the *form vs. content* and *prose vs. poetry* dichotomies, recognizing that if value is in form, characterization is in content, or, more precisely, that in a work of art, prose and poetry are inseparable, as body and soul in living man.

We should then have to begin at the beginning again: what is the content of architecture? What is the content of space? In our photographs there is no content, but in the reality of the architectural imagination and in the reality of buildings content undoubtedly exists. And this is the content: the men who live in architectural space, their actions, indeed their whole physical, psychological and spiritual life as it takes place within it. The content of architecture is its social content.

Architects continually complain about critics who view architecture as a purely plastic creation; but they would complain just as much

220

if the critics, in what would certainly be a step forward, looked at architectural space as one views a ravine or a desert. A large part of the architect's effort is devoted to a building's function, another to the techniques of its structure, a third to its esthetic expression. The very evidence of the phenomenology and genesis of a work of art tells us that there is no point in distinguishing among these three components by separating out *beauty* and ignoring *technique* and *function*. These distinctions are legitimate in philosophy, but they make no sense in the field of criticism, once the co-existence of poetic and non-poetic elements in a work of art has been recognized.

If we center our attention on the interior spaces of architecture and town planning, the indissolubility of social and esthetic problems will appear evident. Is a highway beautiful without automobiles? Is a ballroom beautiful without dancing couples? Isn't the distress, the sense of pain, even the horror that the physio-psychological interpretation attributes to a slight disorganization of plastic elements in the decoration of a dance-hall much greater when we are stifled there and cannot even dance? In a general sense, in judging architecture, can there be a break between social factors, psychological effects, and art?

These questions lead us into the thick of philosophy and esthetics; and for our purpose there is no need to enter this thorny terrain. For in all three of the fundamental categories into which interpretations of the genesis and reality of architecture may be grouped, there is a common element that conditions and determines the validity of each: recognition that space is what counts in architecture and what directs it. This is the answer we set out to seek at the beginning of the chapter.

Political interpretation concerns the basic causes of architectural currents. Granted that an architectural current is not such unless it materializes in space, an *effective* political interpretation of architecture concentrates on spatial tendencies. Philosophical interpretation searches for a synchronism of transcendental or immanent conceptions and those of space. Scientific interpretation insists on architectonic ideas. Obviously, when the socio-economic interpretation maintains that architectural forms derive from economic phenomena, it is reasoning that space expresses particular social customs and culture, which, for economic materialists, are determined by economic conditions. Other positivist interpretations either deal with general phenomena, observe details pertaining to sculpture and painting, or, if they deal with specific architectural facts, concern themselves with spaces. Technical interpretation concerns practical techniques for constructing spaces. We may conclude, in short, that all interpretations based on content make sense in the criticism of architecture to the extent that they center their attention on space.

As to physio-psychological interpretations, we quoted the passage from Geoffrey Scott precisely to show how a keen intelligence, although departing from different premises, must end by identifying the value of architecture with that of its space, to which every other element is subordinate. Interpretations based on the Golden Section, musical harmonic scales, etc., either apply to plastic effects, or, if they are to have architectural validity, must show their adherence to the three-dimensional facts of space. A psychoanalytical interpretation, if it limits itself to volumetric and decorative phenomena, will not go further in the analysis of architecture than Freud's *Moses* in that meager analysis of monotheism. To penetrate far more deeply, it must elucidate the influence of the unconscious on reactions and inhibitions caused by space.

Finally, as to formalist criticism, what does it mean, concretely, to say, as do the formalists, that a building should have unity, proportion, eurhythmy or character? All the arts must have these qualities, and when architecture is the subject, we should specify that it is a question of harmony, proportion or eurhythmy in *spatial* values and of the agreement of all other values with them. Taken literally, even Wölfflin's schemas apply only to architectural or sculptural volumes (not spaces) and their surfaces. If they are to be extended to architecture, new symbols, a new terminology centering on space, must be developed.

We thus arrive at our first conclusion: Spatial interpretation does not compete with other interpretations, because it does not operate on the same plane. It is a super-interpretation, or, if you wish, an underlying-interpretation. More precisely, it is not a specific interpretation like the others, since interpretations of space may be political, social, scientific, technical, physio-psychological, musical and geometric, or formalistic. Contrary to the method current in critical historiography in which the final interpretation (that proposed by the author) demonstrates the error of all preceding interpretations and then replaces them with his own, at the end of our historiographic sketch we wish simply to observe that the ninth and last interpretation, that of space, does not exclude but rather supports the first eight and shows their usefulness in architectural criticism when they are centered on space. Is the philosophic interpretation of architecture true or false? It is true to the extent that it is applied primarily to architectural space. Is the economic interpretation true or false? Again, it is true to the extent that it goes beyond an economic interpretation to become an economic-spatial interpretation. In other words, spatial interpretation is a necessary attribute of every possible interpretation that aims at a deep, concrete and comprehensive view of architecture. It offers us the exact point in architecture where every possible interpretation of art may be applied and by so doing conditions the validity of each interpretation.

Our second conclusion derives from evidence that social content, psychological effects and formal values in architecture all take shape in space. Interpreting space consequently means including all the realities of a building. Every interpretation that does not start with space is constrained to establish that at least one or another aspect of architecture is valueless, and so leaves it out, choosing, *a priori*, a corner of the field on which to concentrate. For example, volumetric and decorative interpretations, which are flourishing widely and freely, particularly exclude all social content from their criticism of architecture.

At this point, it does not concern us to establish a relationship either of identity or of distinction among social content, psychological effects and formal values. There are those who reason about man in terms of the separate areas of the intuitive, logical, practical or ethical without going on from this useful, but theoretical, distinction to the vital, organic unity, the circular wholeness of all the various elements, in whose living combination human and artistic vitality is most exalted. They may be content to ascertain the spatial object of the three categories of interpretation and then continue in their chosen field—social, technical, physio-psychological or formalist—they must take care, however, to recall the hierarchy of architectonic values by which these interpretations become primarily social *and spatial*, technical *and spatial*, physio-psychological *and spatial*, formalist *and spatial*. Those who enter upon more complex inquiry into the organic unity of man and architecture will first agree that their point of departure for an integrated, comprehensive vision of architecture is interpretation of space, and they will measure every element that goes into a building according to the space it encloses.

VI TOWARD A MODERN HISTORY OF ARCHITECTURE

THE CRITICISM of architecture in classic antiquity was much less advanced than that of painting and sculpture. It has remained so in the course of the centuries." So states Lionello Venturi in *The History of Art Criticism* and throughout his book, from Vitruvius to Roger Fry, his opinion is confirmed.

Even recent books on the esthetics of architecture are, for the most part, narrowly empirical, unrelated to contemporary philosophical thought and vague in their theoretical framework. Didactic works of this sort generally champion rules and principles of such flat, grammatical correctness, of such arid anonymity and ingenuous dogmatism, that even the most enthusiastic students can hardly get to the end of them. In the face of their little rules of composition, which omit everything worthwhile in life and art, it is a temptation to fall back on one of the *Sturm und Drang* critics, in revolt against everything which, in the name of fixed, abstract perfection, kills expression and paralyzes vitality. We are tempted to abandon all coldly reasoned systems, intellectual lenses through which we are to view works of art, and to preach hate and love instead. We even want to accept a partial, one-sided criticism, so long as it is able, as Baudelaire has put it, to open great horizons. It becomes preferable to turn occasionally to some old historian, to some pragmatist who is oblivious of our esthetic culture, confused and eclectic in his judgment, but at least enthusiastically responsive to a work of art and at least capable of sincere exclamation, sudden intuition, concrete, psychological appeal. Better the energy of a critical temperament that has at least the humility of submitting to sensation than the niceties of a cold, theoretical approach. In truth, our puritanical attitude, the aristocratic detachment we like to preserve in our esthetic judgment, our mania for philology and documentation and the archeologically fragmentary, dominate the history and criticism of architecture to the point of arousing suspicion that many authors have no passion for their subject or are incapable of spreading, communicating or exciting interest in any emotion they might have.

Our criticism lacks vision and courage. Philologists and connoisseurs are many, but critics are few. Consequently what prevails is conformity; homage to authority and to ready-made opinion; cold, elusive, unarticulated analysis, alien to the impulsiveness of artistic imagination.

In part this is due to art critics, who neglect architecture, who are tied to painting and sculpture by special interests. The value of a painting, in turn, is tied to its commercial value—a canvas of Picasso or a bas-relief of Manzu is raised high in the public mind not only on its own merit, but also because of the buyers and sellers of these canvases and pieces of sculpture, whose prices are largely determined by the critics themselves. Painters of the Ferrarese School rise in price shortly after the appearance of Longhi's book *L'Officina Ferrarese*; Guido Reni drops on the market after his devaluation by modern critics; Delacroix, Chardin and Watteau bring more money than Neo-Classic painters immediately after their "discovery" by the critics. In architecture, however, artistic value is not reflected in a commercial price. Old houses are generally not worth more than modern houses on the market, and a building by Sangallo, Ammannati, Wright, Le Corbusier or Aalto has no higher price because criticism has established it as a work of art. On the economic level, then, we see no relationship between culture and life.

In addition, the archeological spirit, in the negative sense of the term, has established a hiatus between ancient and modern architecture, which is ruinous for the education of the public. No tourist with even a minimum of cultivation, after arriving in London and viewing the old masters in the National Gallery, would neglect going on to the Tate Gallery to admire the Impressionists and the Cubists. But who bothers to visit modern buildings in old tourist centers? How many people who have been to Paris have taken the trouble to see Le Corbusier's Swiss Pavilion in University City? On seeing a painting, there is no one who does not immediately ask, "Who is the artist?"; but the vast majority, even of the highly cultured, feel no need to know the authors of the hundreds of buildings they pass every day. Among the planets of the arts, architecture is the dark side of the moon.

There is an even more important point. By now the coincidence of the history of art and the history of art criticism has been recognized as a cultural fact. Every creative movement brings with it not only works of art, but a taste, a poetry, a school, a way of seeing, which the critic or historian learns to know and on which he ultimately bases his judgment, with which he regards even the productions of the past. In other words, every vital critical position is rooted in an esthetic consciousness determined by the artistic aims of the moment in which it has been developed. As Venturi has remarked, "From the third century before Christ when Xenocrates was writing, up to the time of Winckelmann, the criticism and history of art found their reason for being in the appreciation of contemporary art. Even when the art of the past was studied, it was always judged in relation to the art of the present. Vasari admired Giotto in terms of his contemporary Michelangelo; similarly Bellori admired Raphael and the old masters in the name of Poussin and the Carracci; Mengs admired Raphael, Correggio and Titian in his own name; but Winckelmann reversed this attitude and judged modern art in terms of ancient Greeks. Perfection in art was displaced from the present to the past. The Romantics sought perfection in medieval rather than Greek art, but still in an art of the past. The idealists then drew the logical conclusion from these premises: in the modern era art is dead, because it has been absorbed by scientific philosophy." It was only with French criticism of the last century that we return to a living conception of history, which states, "If it is true that every history is today's interpretation of the past, then awareness of today's art is the basis of every history of the art of the past."

If this by now seems obvious, how many books on architecture are there that are alive with this contemporary consciousness of the history of architecture, in which the author turns to an Egyptian temple or to the monuments of Mycenae with a perception that has been deepened by a knowledge of modern architecture? Is there anyone who is formulating an esthetics of architecture and thus a method of judging the

227

monuments of the past in the light of the contributions of the functionalist movement and of organic architecture? In truth, it appears that the criticism or history of architecture, and its vast number of students and devotees, must be brought up to date by a century to reach today's level of criticism in literature and in painting.

If this cultural need spurs us on to solving the problem of a new history of architecture, there is an opposing and even more substantial need. If it is necessary that modern architecture inform the history of architecture with its spirit of innovation, it is even more vital that a renewed history of architecture contribute to the formation of a higher civilization. A modern critic must goad the public into a vital interest in architecture. He must be as essential to a building and its appreciation as orchestral interpretation is to a score and its listening audience. To come alive, notes marked on the stave by Bach and Debussy wait to be played. Similarly monuments wait, like characters in search of an author, for a modern criticism that will release and reveal them. To clear the ground of historical totems and monumental taboos, to follow art closely in its active creation, to read the works of the past through the eyes of living artists, to judge Borromini with the same willingness and confidence with which a Neutra is judged—all this means throwing open the way not only to modern architecture, but also to the architecture of past centuries.

The culturalistic and archeological prejudices against modern architecture, that stiff, academic attitude we unconsciously adopt when we start to speak about an Alessi rather than a Gropius, as if discussing history required a funeral mask, has a deadly influence that goes beyond the miseducation of merely esthetic taste. Architecture is too bound up with life for its prejudices not to be directly reflected in life. The perspectives of architecture and its criticism are the perspectives of the modern community. It cannot be reiterated too often that so long as the history of architecture fails to burst the bonds of philology and archeology, not only will architecture of the past not acquire the true historicity of current actuality and fail to arouse interest and lively emotion, but the public will continue to believe that architecture is to be found only in monuments, that it is involved only when you build

228

St. Peter's, Rome: Apse by Michelangelo (1547-64), Dome by Michelangelo and G. della Porta (completed 1590) and Colonnade by Bernini (1656-65).

Plate 19. Across the history of architecture

229

Cathedral of Florence (begun in 1296 by Arnolfo di Cambio): Campanile by Giotto, Andrea Pisano and Francesco Talenti (1334-59) and Dome by Brunelleschi (1421-34).

Plate 19. Across the history of architecture

231

Cathedral of Monreale. Interior (1166-89).

F. Ll. Wright: Taliesin, Spring Green, Wis. (1925). Living room.

Plate 19. Across the history of architecture

E. Mendelsohn: Schocken Store, Chemnitz (1928).

Station, Milan (completed 1931). Interior.

Cathedral, Torcello (7th century-1008). Interior.

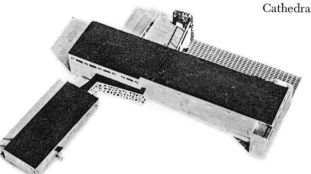

B. Zevi: Community Center,
Cutler, Maine (1940).

Plate 19. Across the history of architecture

233

Montagnana. Aerial view.

Plate 19. Across the history of architecture

234

Farm House, Whitemarsh. Two views.

Plate 20. Across the history of architecture

W. Gropius: Bauhaus, Dessau
(1925). See also pl. 15.

W. W. Wurster: Shuckle Office Building, Sunnyvale, Cal. (1942).

Plate 20. Across the history of architecture

236

F. Borromini: Courtyard of S. Carlino alle Quattro Fontane, Rome (1638-41).

Plate 20. Across the history of architecture

237

Mehmet Aga: Sultan Ahmet Mosque, Istanbul (1609-16). Exterior.

Plate 20. Across the history of architecture

Plate 20. Across the history of architecture

Mehmet Aga: Sultan Ahmet Mosque, Istanbul (1609-16). Interior.

Doges' Palace, Venice (14th-16th century).
Colonnade.

Wladislavski Hall, Prague (1487-1500).

Plate 20. Across the history of architecture

240

"for beauty's sake," and that there is a decided difference between the way you judge a masterpiece of the past and the house you live in, the space of a Byzantine church and the space of the house or apartment in which you are now reading.

Whether we like it or not, we are taking part in a profound change in the way we consider art in relation to life. Aristotle could state that a drama cannot be written with a common man as its hero, but that a noble person of truly heroic scale is required. The modern world, with its balance-sheet of a century of schism between life and culture, of a century of architecture conceived as museum pieces, proclaims exactly the contrary, pledges architects and critics of architecture to their social responsibilities and announces the imminent annihilation of every cultural position that does not serve life, of every artistic activity that remains isolated from the social growth of civilization, and of every way of building that is barren of themes for the bettering of life.

A modern, living, unprejudiced, socially and intellectually useful approach to architecture thus serves not only to prepare us for the esthetic enjoyment of historical works, but also to pose the problem of the social environment in which we live, the urban and architectural spaces in which we spend the greater part of our day, so that we may recognize them and know how to see them.

If you were to wake tomorrow dressed in 18th-century style, you would rub your eyes and wonder whether you had lost your wits or were still dreaming. Only a madman would camouflage a modern automobile as an old coach with a pair of wooden horses on the hood of the motor. Yet most of us live in ridiculous houses, unworthy of man. In fact, any thoughtful, self-respecting man would refuse to vegetate in such houses as are now often provided: stupid little boxes with no conception whatever of space, set up in rows and senselessly coupling a modern kitchen and bath with a living room and bedroom of two or three or four centuries ago. We live in cities that are actively decomposing, where a lack of planning vision has arrested all possibilities for healthy, organic communities, and where speculative building with its murky notion of monumentality is spoiling the sacred places of our spiritual heritage.

A modern, organic history of architecture will not be directed only to the esthetic and intellectual, the cultural and emotional. Beyond the soulless division of Man into economic, emotional and spiritual man, it will speak to the whole, integrated human being. Then we shall see a lifting of the mind's barriers which have confined architectural culture to a moldy, academic corner. Like another sense, we shall acquire a feeling for space, a love of space, and a need for freedom in space. For space, though it cannot in itself determine our judgment of lyrical values, expresses all the factors of architecture—the sentimental, moral, social and intellectual—and thus represents the precise analytical moment of architecture that is material for its history. Space is to architecture-as-art as literature is to poetry; it is the prose of architecture and characterizes each of its works. To put it in terms of formalistic criticism, it is the concrete object of the visual symbols most suitable and adaptable to architecture. This is true principally because it is in space that life and culture, spiritual interest and social responsibility, meet. For space is not merely a cavity, or void, or "negation of solidity"; it is alive and positive. It is not merely a visual fact; it is in every sense, and especially in a human and integrated sense, a reality which we live.

Architecture, as a cultural whole, will flourish again. Capable of distinguishing the authentic from the imitation, the past from the present, our life from the life of yesterday, we shall go to ancient monuments to learn their fundamental lessons in space. In the light of the past and its criticism, theories of contemporary architecture, which with the organic movement already seek to disentangle themselves from the rationalistic formulas of structural "internationalism," shall enrich themselves with an entirely human language.

The need for a modern history of architecture is indicated by all the living factors of the contemporary world: by the collaborative direction of social thinking; by the birth and development of scientific psychology; by the tragic realization, after two World Wars, that the very existence of the documents—the monuments—of our architectural culture depends on the solution of our present problems; by modern figurative criticism; by efforts toward the integration of philosophical thought; by the identification, accepted in theory if not in practice, of

242

culture with our daily way of life; above all by modern architecture, which, in its radical investigation of spatial problems, shows the way for historians and critics to the secret and the reality of architecture.

And so, to be numbered among the promises, hopes, potentialities and tasks of our joint, scholarly undertakings is a new history of architecture, for which these pages on the interpretation of space are intended as but an augury of the future.

BIBLIOGRAPHY

For a general bibliography of theories of art and architecture, see:

BORISAVLJEVIĆ, MILUTIN, *Les Théories de l'Architecture*, Paris, Payot, 1926. The author's uncertain interpretative criteria are revealed in his *Prolégomènes à une Esthétique Scientifique de l'Architecture*, Paris, Fischbacher, 1923.

FELDMAN, VALENTIN, *L'Esthétique Française Contemporaine*, Paris, F. Alcan, 1936.

PELLIZZARI, ACHILLE, *I Trattati attorno le Arti figurative in Italia e nella penisola iberica*, vol. I, Naples, Perrella, 1915; vol. II, Genoa, "Dante Alighieri" [undated].

SCHLOSSER-MAGNINO, JULIUS, *Die Kunstliteratur*, Vienna, Schroll & Col, 1924.

VENTURI, LIONELLO, *History of Art Criticism*, New York, E. P. Dutton & Co., 1936.

Of fundamental importance among books on the theory of architecture is:

SCOTT, GEOFFREY, *The Architecture of Humanism*, New York, Charles Scribner's Sons, 1925; New York, Doubleday Anchor Books, 1954. (Originally London, 1914.)

The following are also outstandingly useful:

FASOLA, GIUSTA NICCO, *Ragionamenti sull' Architettura*, Citta, Macri di Castello, 1949. A compendium of miscellaneous studies, it is also useful for its numerous references to books and articles on the esthetics of architecture.

MOLLINO, CARLO and VADACCHINO, F., *Architettura, Arte e Tecnica,* Turin, Chiantore [undated]. The idealistic thinking of Carlo Mollino is better expressed in his essays, *"Vedere l'architettura,"* published in the magazine, *Agora,* nos. 8, 9-10, 11, Turin, 1946.

PANE, ROBERTO, *Architettura e Arti figurative,* Venice, Pozza, 1948. Of fundamental importance for its essay, "Architettura e letteratura." See Bruno Zevi's review in *Metron,* no. 28, October, 1948.

VITALE, SALVATORE, *L'Estetica dell'Architettura,* Bari, Laterza, 1928. See also *Attualità dell'Architettura,* Bari, 1947, by the same author. Substantial criticisms of this book are expressed by Bruno Zevi in the magazine, *Metron,* nos. 26-27, August-September, 1948, and no. 29, November, 1948.

Our book would not have been possible without the contributions of Nikolaus Pevsner (especially: *An Outline of European Architecture,* London, Pelican Books, 1942, and Scribner, New York, 1948); Lewis Mumford (in particular: *Sticks and Stones,* New York, Norton, 1924, and *The Culture of Cities,* New York, Harcourt Brace, 1938); Italian art critics, notably Carlo Giulio Argan (see his essay, *A proposito di spazio interno,* in *Metron,* no. 28, October, 1948) and Carlo Ludovico Ragghianti (whose book *Ponte a Santa Trinità,* Florence, Vallecchi, 1948, is worth studying); and architects and historians of architecture including Roberto Pane (among other writings, for his *Napoli improvista,* Turin, Einaudi, 1949), Sergio Bettini (particularly for *L'Architettura di San Marco,* Padua, Tre Venezie, 1946), Guglielmo De Angelis d'Ossat, Fausto Franco and in general contributors to the magazine, *Palladio.*

The following are listed and summarized not necessarily because of their notable intrinsic value, but because they are not examined in the bibliographies of the books cited above:

246

ALLSOPP, BRUCE, *Art and the Nature of Architecture*, London, Pitman, 1952.

This essay undertakes to apply to architecture the philosophy expounded by R. G. Collingwood in his *The Principles of Art*. It is an effort similar to many carried out in Italy that aim at applying Croceian esthetics to architecture. Collingwood was, in fact, an admirer and follower of Croce; his thinking is thus easily translated into architectural terms. From the first pages, however, we are faced with the question of whether it is worth the effort. In assimilating architecture with all the arts, an established esthetic truth is reconfirmed, but at the risk of generalization, of not going on to explain the aspects peculiar to each artistic activity. Is it more useful to list the elements common to music, architecture and painting, or to explore their internal reality, to underline their distinctive characteristics? In Italy, the answer to these questions was provided by Croce himself, who, while firmly rejecting the theory of the separation of the arts, maintained "the opportuneness of composing theoretical books on the separate arts" (*La Poesia*, p. 186), and demonstrated the concrete utility of this approach in the field of literature. In England, however, general premises have not yet been developed in specific critical areas.

This short book is divided into four parts. In the first, which is devoted to an adequate summation of the basic ideas of modern esthetics, the author proposes a distinction between craft and art, the one characterized as a means to a predetermined end, the other independent and fully grasped only in the process of creation. The distinction is similar to that drawn by Croce between literature and poetry, which several of the authors cited have carried over into the distinction between building and architecture.

The second part goes into the themes of functionality, style, tradition and the needs set by contemporary creativity in connection with the *originality versus tradition* conflict. The author criticizes mechanistic and utilitarian theories of architecture, upholds the modern idiom, but postulates its link with tradition without, however, singling out what could make this link possible. Since he does not characterize modern architecture historically, it remains one style among the many of the past, and valid recommendation relapses into abstract theory.

The third part, after confirming the unity of the arts and the relative value to be assigned to the special qualities and limits of the various arts, takes up the argument of architectural teaching in its intellectual, technical and artistic phases. Here the author's intention becomes a little more illuminating (p. 94): "In architectural education . . . it is clear that a student must learn how to make himself understood. He must, in fact, learn the ways of doing things that are understood. That is one aspect of his technique. Obviously history will be the most important technical subject he has to study." P. 99: "Art is a kind of language. The grammar of a language is not a set of irrevocable rules, it is merely a statement of common usage and is changing all the time in any living language. Knowing the vocabulary and grammar, in other words the technique of the language, helps us when we want to say something . . ." But in what does this technique really consist? P. 100: "An architect's technique must be a knowledge of the history of art. But he cannot know all its history—all about all the architecture there has ever been. He will naturally tend to concentrate upon certain periods. Some architects have limited themselves to Gothic or Renaissance architecture, others to what they call contemporary, which is a bad name for recent history. Both extremes limit the designer. The latter may limit him to the fashions of the moment, the former may preclude the expression of feelings possible only to a modern man." All this is proper, but scarcely penetrating, since it does not touch the necessity of rewriting the whole history of instruction in architectural design, that is, the theme of a methodological revision of architectural teaching, but stops with the juxtaposition of ancient and modern, auguring a better balance in future historical treatments.

The conclusion of this book is a defense of individuality in the architectural profession and of the value of art. With somewhat ingenuous enthusiasm the author states (p. 119): "There is nothing inherently impossible in the idea that all buildings should be architecture when we know, as we do, that any building can be . . . Fine design does not cost more; it may even save money. We shall have it when we believe it matters."

BRADDELL, DARCY, *How to Look at Buildings*, London, Methuen & Co 1932.
Based on the findings of Belcher and Edwards, this book has the

merit of facing, though reluctantly, some of the problems of modern architecture. Space, however, is ignored; consequently this book does not go much beyond earlier critical ones. What are the qualities of architecture here? 1) Expression, in the plastic expressionistic sense of the word; 2) composition, in which the author distinguishes the picturesque from the formal approach; 3) proportion, in which the ordered proportion of the classic is distinguished from the instinctive proportion of the romantic; 4) scale, which is well exemplified empirically; 5) detail, which provides the author with an opportunity to discuss critically the negative position of the functionalists; 6) ornament; 7) texture, that is, the grain, the tactile values, of materials; 8) color; 9) civic sense, in which the concepts of Edwards' *Good and Bad Manners in Architecture* (q.v.) are repeated.

BRAGDON, CLAUDE, *The Beautiful Necessity*, New York, Alfred A. Knopf, 1949.

Of all books dealing with "laws" of architectonic beauty, this is certainly the most original. Starting from an avowed theosophic faith, the author affirms that art is an expression of cosmic life revealing itself in natural laws of which the artist may be unaware, but which are permanent in all his work.

Within the framework of the arts, two poles are formed by music and architecture. The first exists essentially in time, the second in space. The famous remark that architecture is frozen music is (p. 15) "a poetical statement of a philosophical truth, since that which in music is expressed by means of harmonious intervals of time and pitch, successively, after the manner of time, may be translated into corresponding intervals of architectural void and solid, height and width." Music is dynamic, subjective, intellectual and one-dimensional; architecture is static, objective, physical and three-dimentional. A historical survey follows in which forms of every period are interpreted as symbolic of the thought of the period; this closes the first chapter, which is perhaps the least interesting of the book.

Unity here is the first law of architecture. The second is *polarity:* everything has gender, either feminine or masculine; in architecture we find a continual contact between the masculine (simple, direct, positive, primary, active) and the feminine (indirect, complex, derivative,

249

passive, negative). P. 32: "Things hard, straight, fixed, vertical, are Yo [masculine]; things soft, curved, horizontal, fluctuating, are In [feminine]." The column is masculine, the architrave feminine; the abacus masculine, the echinus feminine; the triglyphs masculine, the metopes feminine; a tower is masculine, a flat roof feminine.

The third law is *trinity:* masculine and feminine elements in contact tend toward a third thing which is neuter. Product of the two architectonic factors—the vertical and the horizontal—is the arch. The fourth law is *consonance:* the microcosm is an echo and repetition of the macrocosm; the triglyphs are the echo of the Doric column; Brunelleschi's dome echoes in the cupolas below. In other words: repetition with variation. *Diversity in monotony* is the fifth law. The beauty of medieval arcades depends on the fact that in a mechanical scheme there are variations, even though imperceptible. *Balance* is the sixth law, while the seventh consists of *rhythmic change:* as a human finger goes from base to tip in rhythmic diminuendo, so the Greek column is rhythmically attenuated, and this explains entasis. The last law, *radiation,* harks back to the primary law of the universe with its directing lines.

"The Bodily Temple" is the title of the chapter following, which applies anthropometric theories to plans and elevations. Then "Latent Geometry" illustrates cases in which strict geometric composition, simple figures, underlie architectonic forms. "The Arithmetic of Beauty" seeks numerical laws in architecture and the final chapter, "Frozen Music," shows how proportions in architecture may be translated into musical phrases corresponding to basic scales.

Fully illustrated, the book, within the limits of its aims, is stimulating and unquestionably diverting.

BRAGDON, CLAUDE, *Architecture and Democracy*, New York, Alfred A. Knopf, 1918. (2nd edition, 1926)

After the comments above on *The Beautiful Necessity*, which was published subsequently, little remains to be said about this book so far as interpretations of architecture are concerned. Here architectural themes of democracy are sought, but beyond architecture as expression, the discussion involves building types, democratic, urbanistic control of building. The architecture of American democracy in 1918 could not have had abstract principles, for a sensitive critic like Bragdon, but only a great artistic personality as inspiration: Louis H. Sullivan. The essay on this architect is the most exciting part of the book.

Also noteworthy is the distinction the author makes between what he calls the two orders of architecture: the "arranged" and the "organic." Arranged architecture is rational and artificial, produced by talent and governed by taste. Organic architecture is (p. 54) "The product of some obscure inner necessity for self-expression which is subconscious." Arranged architecture is created and not creative, imagined but not imaginative. Organic architecture is created and creative, non-Euclidean (p. 55) "in the sense that it is higher-dimensional—that is, it suggests extension in directions and into regions where the spirit finds itself at home, but of which the senses give no report to the brain." Bragdon's philosophy of the organic is rich with important motives, though very different from the theoretical framework of Organic architecture as formulated many years afterward.

BUTLER, ARTHUR S. G., *The Substance of Architecture*, London, Constable & Co., 1926 (and 1932).

The scanty philosophical preparation of the author leads him into prolix divagations on the difference between physical, scientific and esthetic pleasures, into uncertain definitions of architecture as an art balancing artistic and practical requirements, in short, into a pragmatism bestrewn with quasi-persuasive "fairness." As a critic, he lacks perspective, the result of his eclectic taste. His characterizations of the few buildings illustrated, which should exemplify a critical method, apart from some acute observations (for example, those on the Ca' d'Oro in Venice), are not convincing.

His search for a method of looking at buildings is, however, significant. Architectonic beauty, states the author, concerns "the appearance of a building," and then the question is put: "But how do we see it?" (p. 35). Without the capacity of a unitary spatial or volumetric vision, the answer is predictable: very few buildings are built so as to give the same effect from every point of view, and even these do not achieve their goal because, for example, the Baptistry of Pisa "being quite round and—as it were—smooth all over . . . the eye . . . circulates indefinitely in pursuit of complete satisfaction" (p. 37). Better examples are the Radcliffe Library at Oxford and the church of S. Maria della Salute in Venice, where a specific entrance point may be seen. "May we not then conclude that all buildings of any character have one aspect which dominates all other aspects, one appearance which clings to the memory longer than the others whether it be an internal or an external one . . ." (p. 28). With this fine rule established, the casuistry begins: Hagia Sophia signifies its interior, the Cathedral of Reims its façade; for Chartres the author is in some doubt, but then decides that "the aspect of the outside . . . is its dominant one." He concludes (p. 41): "Firstly . . . all buildings have more than one appearance, even those which like the average London house have only one visible front. We can always find, however, some point of view—some angle or elevation—from which such a front looks best. Secondly, from all the possible appearances or views of a building with two sides we can select one aspect in which the two sides appear in happiest combination; and a good photographer does this intuitively. Thirdly, there is always a point at which to stand in a room where the three visible walls, the floor and ceiling appear with the maximum effect."

This inability to see architecture naturally leads to such theories that separate a building and its spatial factors, laying them out in static images and two-dimensional pictures. The real problem is avoided. Instead of judging architecture, a point of view is chosen, the building is photographed from it, and then the photograph, rather than the building, is described.

BYRON, ROBERT, *The Appreciation of Architecture*, London, Wishart & Co., 1932.

This interesting work bases architectural judgment on distinguishing between two categories of building: 1) static architecture, whose principal concern is the affirmation of symmetry and balance, the coordination of all elements with respect to a focal point—a type characteristic of the Mediterranean; 2) mobile architecture, more romantic and at the same time more functional, in which the visual directives are centrifugal.

A series of examples follow, including: Palladio's La Rotonda ("static composition achieved by symmetry, balance and calculated ratios"), Gothic churches ("mobile composition achieved by a profusion of vertical lines"), St. Peter's, Rome ("static elements combined in mobile panorama"), Hagia Sophia ("alliance of the static and the mobile"). It should be added that the author also analyzes elements of mobility that exist in static compositions and *vice versa*. His concept concerns the dominance of one category or the other, not their exclusive affirmation.

CLOZIER, RENÉ, *L'Architecture, éternel livre d'images,* Paris, Laurens, 1948.

Despite its appearance of greater critical agility, this book falls into the general category of French manuals: full of clichés and a vague psychology that fails to conceal a fundamental lack of ideas and critical perspective. Not by chance has it been awarded a prize by the French Academy.

Original influences in architecture, the author says, are three: 1) the nature of the terrain; 2) the exigencies of the climate; 3) human needs. An architectonic conception, determined by these influences, takes visible form through: 4) the decision resulting from the choice of one among the many possible solutions; 5) the composition, which expresses the decision taken, arranging its constituent elements in a harmonious way; 6) the proportions, whose laws complete those of the composition in that they determine the sizes of the different parts of the composition which stemmed from the decision; 7) human scale (the author maintains that the Greco-Roman world was ignorant of human scale, which, he says, constituted the great contribution of the Christian era and characterized French architecture up to and through the Renaissance); 8) values and location, that is, the focus of the composition (the element dominating all others) and the unalterable relationship between nature and the building; and 9) the technical possibilities of execution.

So-called general principles that attempt empirically to harmonize apparently opposed requirements follow: 10) convenience and esthetics ("the esthetics of a construction are but the harmonic expression of its functionality"); 11) harmony and a "considered symmetry" must be sought; 12) simplicity and poverty, which resolves (or better, avoids) the problem by preaching "a richness that remains modest;" 13) logic and feeling, where the author establishes (it is easily anticipated) that "architecture results from the perfect equilibrium of logic and feeling;"

253

14) internationalism and regionalism (regionalism means the adaptation of a style to a definite place, and consequently internationalism constitutes the evolution of culture and regionalism its stability); 15) construction and decoration, which naturally are also not "in opposition, but complete each other" in that decoration "expresses structure;" 16) style and the styles ("style is the very essence of architecture, while styles are its classification"); the styles divide into higher styles (Egyptian, Greek and Gothic) and secondary styles (Roman, Byzantine and the styles from the Renaissance to our own day), distinguished by the fact that in secondary styles decoration does not express construction, but only covers it.

The book closes with a very flat survey of architectural styles. It unwittingly proves once again how bankrupt is an attempt such as this to create a particular "esthetics of architecture" and how absurd to search for the laws of architectural composition outside the concrete history of architecture, outside, that is, the specific characterization of its personalities and monuments.

EDWARDS, TRYSTAN, *Good and Bad Manners in Architecture*, London, Philip Alan & Co., 1924; reprinted by Tiranti, Ltd., London 1945.

Written in a pragmatic, almost experimental, tone, free of "principles" and opposed to any sort of critical obscurantism, Edwards' short book begins with a chapter on "Civic Values," condemning the mania of competition between city buildings, which has replaced the instinctive coordination in building cities in former times: "A few people standing up here or there in a theater audience might get a better view of the stage, but if they all stood up they would not be better off than before. If one or two attempted to infringe this rule they would be promptly told to sit down" (p. 14). The rule of urbanity is synonymous with good manners, or proper behavior, in town planning. In our time the commercial, publicity-seeking drive joins forces with monumentality: every building tries to be exceptional—and this is what Edwards means by "bad manners in architecture." If monumentality is bad manners in town planning, it is also architectural immorality in that it does not respect human scale, but depresses the spectator and makes him feel Lilliputian. What distinguishes a Regency row of shops from a modern row is the *sociability* of the former, its having been thought out and built to attract and invite man, not to glorify big business. In the hierarchy of the arts, established by Edwards in a previous book, *The Things Which Were Seen* (Philip Alan & Co., London, 1921), the beauty of the human body is pre-eminent, good manners follow, then the art of dressing, then architecture, and finally painting and sculpture. Consequently it is natural that he should consider *charm* to be a fundamental quality of architecture, and feel that urban building, as "a member of society," must follow specific rules of decorum, like a man in a drawing-room. No arrogance, megalomania, monumentality; no ostentation in proportion, color or pose. Edwards' book is a manual of "how to live architecturally."

With a modest critical vocabulary—*appealing, polite, amiable, pleasant, varied, attractive*—and a pleasing, informal conversational flow, the second chapter examines the original and present character of Regent Street in London, the work of the famous architect, John Nash. Using examples, it marvellously illustrates the presumptuous and bombastic building which has replaced what was formerly intelligent, urbane, cordial, "desirous of pleasing rather than impressing."

"The Bugbear of Monotony" (title of the third chapter) lashes out at the obsession for originality, diversity, eccentricity and "personality," in building. From it, he says, is derived the extreme tedium of the ensemble of these romantic architectural idiosyncrasies. A succession of different and strident colors results in the deadly effect of uniformity; decorations of little porches, marble and travertine dados, cornices of various types, do not produce lively variety, but only boring disorder. The author looks, fundamentally, to what we might call *volumetric town planning*. (Which would be more monotonous—one hundred men dressed in different colors or one hundred men wearing an accepted type of evening dress? If elegant clothes are standardized, this means that a certain social distinction is recognized in uniformity. The Georgian style, without arriving at complete equality, avoided the vulgarity of a compounded romanticism and led to variety within a common cultural standard.)

Going on to study Ruskin's principle of *truth*, the author affirms that, as the art of living is not in unbridled expression, but in knowing how to say some things and passing others in silence, so the art of architecture must suppress some half-truths in homage to larger truths. The verity of a building, like that of a man, may be both polite and vulgar. The problem of good manners is that of expressing the first and hiding the second.

Edwards' position may be defined as psychological. His book would be particularly useful if read by monumentalistic architects and by those with a neurotic interest in "originality" at all costs; for the character of urban sociability which Edwards emphasizes is among the most important requisites of good architecture. About the problem of space, the author says nothing; his book does not concern the body or the structure, but only the clothing, of architecture. Within these limits, it is perfectly achieved.

EDWARDS, TRYSTAN, *Style and Composition in Architecture,* London, John Tiranti Ltd., reprinted 1945.

The author begins with the statement that the beautiful is the organic, whatever has an organized physical structure like that found in animals and plants. A distinction is then made between style and character, and a comparison between the concepts of language and style. The primary aim of this book is to supply a grammar of design. According to the author (p. 21), design is "governed by three main principles, those of Number, Punctuation, and Inflection. The whole form of architecture is included therein, and everything else appertaining to a building which cannot be interpreted in terms of these principles belongs to the subject of architecture." (The subject is the argument treated in the other book by Edwards reviewed above.) P. 25: "The function of designing the visual arts is to imbue inanimate objects with the qualities of life," and these organic qualities are given in architecture through the principles listed above.

Number is discussed by analysis of a long series of typical buildings compared with animal organisms. The qualities of unity, duality and trinity are treated in this chapter; however, it deals only with the composition of façades.

Punctuation is defined (p. 51) as a "process of design by which one can give to any object a certain consciousness of its own extremities," accentuating its limits; this is largely an analysis of emphasis extended to the entire façade of a building.

The canon of *Inflection* is defined as "the principle which governs the relation of the parts of an object to the whole and the relation of that whole to what lies outside." The major part of this section is an analysis of proportions.

A chapter follows on the application of the three canons to planimetrics, then there is a chapter on scale and proportion, and a long discussion of ornament.

As will be evident, this short book on architectonic grammar is not so interesting as its psychological equivalent, *Good and Bad Manners in Architecture*. When an author, however, is lively and acute, as here, even a brief disquisition on grammar turns out to be stimulating.

GREELEY, WILLIAM ROGER, *The Essence of Architecture*, New York, D. Van Nostrand Co., 1927.

Magnificently illustrate any book on architecture and its value is thereby enhanced. The illustrations are not, however, the only merit of Greeley's book. Within the framework of traditional esthetics, this is unquestionably one of the finest treatises, if only for its experimental approach that avoids the boring and pedantic tone of books of this kind, as well as the schoolroom casuistry typified by Gormort's work (see below).

The author starts from a distinction between the descriptive and the non-descriptive arts, the latter including architecture, music and the dance, then, with regard to architecture, establishes a difference between qualities of "background" (content) and those of the figurative.

Geography, tradition, history, race and character of people constitute the background elements.

Architectural composition must obey four principles: sincerity, propriety, style, scale; the difference between sincerity and propriety is effectively expounded. Other characteristics of composition are: unity, balance, emphasis, proportion. A final chapter deals with the characteristics of picturesque architecture. On space, there is not one word.

However, the book is useful, because the author, even when expressing a dubious opinion, seeks to weigh it experimentally.

GROMORT, GEORGES, *Initiation à l'Architecture*, Collection "Manuels d'Initiation," Paris, Librairie d'Art R. Cucher, 1938.

Of all the scholastic manuals on the esthetics of architecture, this work is perhaps the best. Bearing in mind the teachings of Geoffrey Scott's *The Architecture of Humanism* and John Belcher's *Essentials in Architecture,* the author avoids the common defects of this kind of book. Compare it, however, with Matteo Marangoni's *The Art of Seeing Art* (London, Shelley Castle, 1951), by now a classic introduction to the figurative arts, to see how backward architectural criticism has remained.

The author sets out by dividing the field of architecture into three traditional sectors: structural solidity, practical utility and beauty. Then he goes on with categories of architectural beauty: 1) unity, 2) contrast, 3) symmetry, 4) proportion, 5) geometrical and mathematical proportions, and 6) the esthetic values of the theme of honesty and truth. Chapters on the composition of plans and façades follow. He continues with: 7) character, 8) scale, 9) architectural and sculptural decoration, 10) simplicity and sobriety, 11) style and 12) material. This completes the first part, which is followed by two very brief sections on moldings and the classic orders, and on the evolution of forms and structures.

The usefulness of this book does not depend on any clear interpretation that it provides, but on the abundance of its illustrations and on its tone of good common sense, which implies that all judgment is almost always a half-truth. The author takes into account many kinds of artistic creation, and this completeness makes his work valuable. It could be given to the layman as an introductory book on architecture, if prefaced as follows: "This is an encyclopedia of architectural categories. Remember, however, that architecture begins with the elimination of these categories. If criticism is to have any utility, it must be that of illuminating *with passion* some aspect of architecture, some truth, partial though it may be. The author, on the other hand, has taken *liqueurs* of criticism, mixed them together and watered them down; the result: his esthetics of architecture."

GROMORT, GEORGES, *Essai sur la Théorie de l'Architecture*, Paris, Vincent Fréal, 1946.

With a wealth of magnificent illustrations, this large volume repeats, in a diluted form, concepts expressed in the smaller book, *Initia-*

tion à l'Architecture, described above; and its didactic pronouncements, almost like those of a handbook on architectural composition, render this treatment more dangerous than the earlier one. Gromort's effort is to analyze the greatest possible number of works, to extract common architectonic principles from them, and to show how these are permanently valid in design. It is an old and discredited effort, ignorant of the fact that the teaching of architecture can be based only on historical criticism, and not on abstract games of proportion and scale. The Beaux-Arts school founded its teaching on classical principles of composition; the modern functionalist school, on the abstract compositional principles of post-Cubist movements in painting. A preliminary architectural education based on modern historical criticism is a compelling need for our universities. Much of the philological material prepared by the Beaux-Arts schools can be utilized; even Gromort's book is rich with interesting information. But the theoretical groundwork of the Beaux-Arts schools must be radically changed.

GUTTON, ANDRÉ, *Conversation sur l'architecture,* vol. I, Paris, Vincent Fréal, 1952.

The first part of a work in several volumes, this book constitutes the esthetic premise for a weighty treatise that proposes to examine various types of building (from the private house to the theater and courthouse) and the problems inherent in town planning. A true and proper encyclopedia of architecture, like the one prepared very recently in America by Talbot Hamlin (*Forms and Functions of 20th Century Architecture,* 4 vols., New York, Columbia University Press, 1952), it has all the defects common to this kind of work. Hamlin pragmatically devoted his second volume to "principles of composition," reserving the first for "constructive elements" and the last two for "types of building." Gutton, on the other hand, follows the custom of giving precedence to the problems of art and the architectural profession.

The most useful feature here is the original selection of photographs. For the prolix text as a whole, the comments made above on René Clozier's book might be repeated: dearth of ideas and method, vague psychological approximations and, what is particularly irritating, an interminable series of self-evident statements pronounced with a tone of discovery and academic earnestness.

259

Why, we must ask, are these defects typical of recent French works?

Does it perhaps go back to 1675, when François Blondel created the first course in "The Theory of Architecture" at the *École Nationale Supérieure des Beaux-Arts*? The program of that course was divided into two parts: the first, dedicated to the analysis of "primary elements" (walls, orders, arcades, windows, etc.) and "complex elements" (rooms, entries, stairs, courtyards, etc.); the second, to general principles of composition and various types of religious, civil, military, public and private building. In 1901, Julien Guadet published his famous *Eléments et Théorie de l'architecture,* conceived on the basis of the course he gave in 1894; this work was preceded by J.-B. Lesueur's *Histoire et Théorie de l'Architecture,* in 1879, and was followed by a myriad of similar books, from Leonce Reynaud's *Traité d'architecture* to Jean Rondelet's *Traité* and A. Vaillant's *Théorie de l'architecture* in 1919.

The great lack in these treatises, beginning with Guadet's, is methodological in nature and consists of the following fallacies: a) that architecture derives from the resolution of its simple and complex "elements" and that it may accordingly be divided critically and didactically into a series of empirical problems; b) that architectural treatises are to be conceived according to kinds and types of building; c) that architectural "theory" is something different from the history of architecture, on which it continually relies, but only to extract "universally valid principles" from it.

Gutton's book does not escape the manifold consequences of these fallacies, and the reservations expressed here and there concerning the possibility of holding to strict rules of composition do not serve to raise the discussion to a more realistic level. Instead, they weaken the persuasive force of the old assumptions that are accepted fundamentally, but without the rigor that makes Guadet's preconceptions interesting and, at any rate, significant of a culture and a way of creation. Gutton admits subscribing to the ideas expressed in Gromort's books, and aims to complete his study of buildings in relation to their setting in the city and on the landscape. The environmental theme is actually present throughout the rather monotonous text, but is not carried to any conclusion, because of the methodological uncertainties mentioned above. Even a "theory" of town planning cannot be achieved, despite the abundance of examples shown, if it is not identified with the specific history of the city discussed.

HAMLIN, TALBOT FAULKNER, *The Enjoyment of Architecture*, New York, Duffield & Co., 1916. (Scribner, 1921)

This book begins with the consideration (p. 20) that "the number of emotions architecture can produce is limited." It cannot express love; it expresses: 1) power, 2) peace or repose, 3) gaiety, playfulness or relaxation. "Every building, every well-designed room should carry in itself at least one message of cheer or rest or power."

Concerning the "laws of architecture": unity, variety, balance, rhythm, good proportion, center of interest, harmony. Resulting from these laws is the fact (p. 69) that "every beautiful building [has] a threefold composition, a beginning, middle and end."

The second chapter is devoted to the materials of architectonic expression: walls, roofs, doors, windows, chimneys. It contains statements such as these (p. 74): "The appeal of a building to the senses is produced by two things only, the play of light and shade over its varied surfaces, and the colour of the materials of which it is composed," or (p. 77) in "brick walls . . . there must be quiet repose."

The book continues with a very long chapter on ornament and its criticism, a section on plans, another on the meaning of style, and finally a chapter on the social value of architecture. Although fairly comprehensive, the author is oblivious to the difference between the Classic and the Neo-Classic, Gothic and Neo-Gothic, a work of art and its copy. For this reason, many of the examples given are entirely gratuitous.

LEATHART, JULIAN, *Style in Architecture*, London, Thomas Nelson & Sons, 1940.

Despite its title, this is a positivist (technical and climatological) interpretation of architecture. Written by a modern architect, it has the merit of giving a view of the history of architecture from its origins to the present day. An interesting chapter discusses "The Modern Romantic Style," which is supposed to follow the functionalist period.

LYON, THOMAS HENRY, *Real Architecture*, Cambridge, W. Heffer & Sons, 1932.

An unpretentious book, aimed at illustrating the commonest errors of clients and architects: 1) the difference between good architecture and a fine pictorial rendering of a building; 2) the problem of the architect's personality; 3) sentimental confusion about setting and environment; 4) the romanticism of "antiquing" and of creepers on buildings; 5) the preconception that natural materials are the most beautiful; 6) the preconception that handicraft production is better than industrial; 7) the false idea that "true" architecture was created only when the architect was also the builder. The aim of the book is carried out with finesse, from the point of view of an admirer of the English 18th century, particularly of the Georgian style.

NEWTON, WILLIAM GODFREY, *Prelude to Architecture*, London, The Architectural Press, 1925.

The spatial theme is mentioned (p. 13): "[Architecture] is to be considered in terms of cube measure. We take a piece of space and hedge it round and cover it in." The reference is fleeting, however. Written in the free and easy style of the modern architect, this slim volume criticizes the Beaux-Arts thesis of "the expression of the plan," then criticizes the functionalist thesis of "the expression of structure" (p. 18): "The human body, with its hints of muscle and bone and sinew at nodal points, expresses its structure without revealing it." Then there is a discussion of the stylistic approach that is based on the "correctness of the archeological echo" and the casual statement is made (p. 26) that: "It is all to the good that we should begin to think of buildings from the inside outwards rather than from the outside in." The author hits at the ignorance of functionalists who believe that utility and structure determine form, and he makes fun of them, quoting (p. 52) "the story of the king who, desiring to find out what was the original language of mankind, took two new-born babies from their parents and had them suckled by goats, until they were of an age when speech might be expected; then they were brought before the king, and all men attended to see what would come of the experiment. But all the little ones could do was bleat." Easy and amusing to read, the book closes with a plea for the necessity of poetic creation.

PAKINGTON, HUMPHREY, *How the World Builds*, London, Black, 1949.

Revision of the original text (1932) has not improved this work.

three-quarters of it composed of a pedestrian historical survey and completed by two chapters on the theory and enjoyment of architecture. The statement (p. 88) that "History is the story of the facts, the dry bones: the theory breathes life into those dry bones, shows us how to see beauty in the form," indicates the limits of this approach, unpardonable even in a popular work. Then follows the usual list of ingredients for architectural beauty: *proportion,* about which, however, the author expresses some reserve (p. 89): "the Parthenon is a perfectly proportioned building in marble . . . But recently an exact copy of the Parthenon was erected in America in ferro-concrete. Here the proportions looked the same, but were in fact quite wrong; for ferro-concrete beams would naturally be spaced more widely than would stone columns carrying stone beams, owing to the strength of the steel embedded in the concrete . . . the rules of proportion are different owing to the different materials used. So if proportion depends on materials the question cannot be settled by the eye; for the eye cannot see the skeleton of the building"; *contrast, harmony, rhythm, balance, "unresolved duality"* (according to which, as a nose and a mouth exist in the center of a human face, so it is necessary to have in the middle of a symmetrical façade an architectural element that attracts attention), and *scale.* The author provides highly dubious examples of all these qualities in schematic sketches; for instance, to illustrate the quality of *contrast,* he draws a round dome and a neighboring spire. The student might properly ask whether this composition does not correspond more to *harmony* and *rhythm;* otherwise he must conclude that S. Maria della Salute in Venice is not good architecture, because its two domes are not in contrast.

POND, IRVING K., *The Meaning of Architecture,* Boston, Marshall Jones & Co., 1918.

To succeed in digesting a long series of books on the esthetics of architecture is possible only if one has the optimistic conviction that in the worst of them there is at least one intelligent observation, one allusion to the truth. This conviction is confirmed even in this book, in which the author, in effect, declares: "It is soon said what architecture is: the Greek temple!"

The Greek temple is perfection. Egypt is quite off the track, Rome is plagiaristic, the Gothic a little better, the Renaissance terrible—these are the historical theses of the book. Pond follows with an anthropomorphic interpretation of the Greek orders, in which the Doric is defined as "man," the Ionic as "woman," and the Corinthian as "decadence." In the chapter on "Significance of Mass and Form," the physio-psychological effect of different geometric forms is illustrated and this is perhaps the most interesting section, despite its conclusions: on the plain, building should be vertical (Egypt); in hilly regions, horizontal lines should predominate (Greece)—this is true, however, only in countries with clear skies (Greece and Egypt), which should adopt simple forms. In countries with cloudy skies, when the terrain is flat—pyramidal forms (Gothic in England); when it is mountainous—cubic masses (medieval castles in France). The study of the relationship between racial and architectural profiles is amusing, if superficial, as is the chapter on rhythm, based on the relations between architecture and the dance.

From the premises, one would expect a concluding criticism of the modern (1918) style that would be an apology for the Greek Revival, but the author unexpectedly rejects it in favor of an entirely symbological Art Nouveau.

ROBERTSON, HOWARD, *The Principles of Architectural Composition,* London, The Architectural Press, 1924.

If this book, written in 1924, had been confined to its first edition, its inadequacies would be understandable; but a fourth edition was published in 1945, and it is used as a textbook for architectural composition in some schools of the British Empire. Accordingly, it must be judged not only empty, like so many others, but decidedly harmful. By 1945 a mature philosophy and criticism of space had been developed, and there were at least ten books that, in one way or another, clearly explained the spatial essence of architecture. The author, though listing some of these books in his bibliography, takes no account of space.

Unity, composition of masses, the element of contrast—he says—are the laws of architecture; there follow, as secondary principles, emphasis, expression of character, proportion, scale. Laws and principles are broadly exemplified, and often in a highly questionable way, using only façades and volumes. There are, finally, a chapter on the composition of plans, purely formal and academic; a discussion on the relationship between plan and elevation, in which the author does

264

not take a position; and a superficial treatment of the expression of function in buildings.

This is a fairly typical example of how most architectural theoreticians have remained twenty years behind in esthetic and critical thinking, oblivious of the creative contributions of modern architecture. The author cites two examples by Le Corbusier and Wright. These turn out to be Le Corbusier's first villa, symmetrical in plan, and Wright's Imperial Hotel in Tokyo!

ROBERTSON, HOWARD, *Architecture Explained,* London, Ernest Benn, 1926.

Written by a practicing architect, this book is much stronger in structure and interest than those given to the casuistries of abstract beauty. After a rapid review of historical periods, there are three chapters dedicated to principles of design. Then follows a chapter on "Character in Architecture," which is valuable even within its expressionistic limits. The book closes with a panorama of modern architecture. Informed with a practicing and anti-archeological mentality, it makes pleasant reading.

ROBERTSON, MANNING and NORA, *Foundations of Architecture,* London, Edward Arnold & Co., 1929.

"This book embodies an attempt to analyse its [architecture's] elements in a manner that should appeal as a foundation for an adult as well as for a child at the secondary school stage," say the authors in the preface. In fact, the book is of little use even to a high school student. In its chapters on various materials from brick to reinforced concrete, on the house, on details and decoration, on color; and even in the chapter devoted to proportion and the grouping of masses, the most obvious and thus the most arbitrary concepts are repeated. "Everything is simple and natural," is the tone of the authors. Unfortunately everything here is vague and so not quite true.

RUTTER, FRANK, *The Poetry of Architecture,* Hodder & Stoughton, London; New York, George H. Doran Co., 1924.

Having stated that architecture is "an effect of which building is the cause," or "building touched with emotion," the author proceeds to a historical classification of this emotional content, defining Egyptian

265

architecture as that of "fear," Greek as that of "grace," etc., and succeeds only in producing vague psychological characterizations that could be applied as well to an ugly copy as to an authentic monument. Architectonic forms, in this rather crudely symbolistic interpretation, become the translation of philosophical attitudes. Despite some penetrating observations, the book has the same defects as all those that paraphrase Ruskin without having the exalted passion which alone justified his excesses.

STURGIS, RUSSELL, *How to Judge Architecture*, New York, The Baker & Taylor Co., 1903.

This book is mentioned here only because of the significance of the title. It is a true and proper *history* of architecture, but because the author apparently sought to avoid a professorial tone and adopted instead an almost colloquial style, he thought it wiser not to call it a history. The same thing seemed to have occurred to Lewis Mumford when he (or his publisher) called a book of his *Sticks and Stones,* in reality a splendid history of American architecture. This indicates how little American public opinion is attracted by the word and the concept of *history* (an understandable aversion, in view of the fact that most historiography is written with an antiquarian, archeological or philological nostalgia).

THOMAS, MARK HARTLAND, *Building Is Your Business*, London, Wingate, 1947.

Of the four chapters that make up this elegant book, which aims at informing the public on building activity, the first concerns the definition of specialists (architect, engineer, builder, "quantity surveyor" [estimator of costs], etc.); the second, building technics (various materials and mechanical equipment of a house, to which are added two paragraphs on modular design); the fourth examines the architect's professional activity as it has developed in modern times. Only the third chapter, titled "Architecture as an Art," offers critical definitions and is completed by an illustrated appendix. Here we find brief but intelligent pronouncements. Pp. 72-73: "Architecture is a three-dimensional art. Like sculpture it is not primarily concerned with the external shape of things, although of course the form of buildings as seen from outside, in the abstract, is an important element of architecture. There is an overlap here between sculpture and architecture. For example, a commemorative monument may be designed by an architect or by a sculptor: it was a sculptor who designed the famous H. M. V. electric iron, but an architect designed 'Ekco' radio cabinets . . . Though an architect's experience in handling three-dimensional form makes him a useful member of a team to design anything from a city down to a teacup, architecture itself is the application of form to a particular purpose— the enclosure of space . . . Architecture, the art of spatial enclosure . . . is the act of humanizing substantial parcels of infinity, and bringing them within man's reach and understanding." More debatable is his thesis according to which man encloses space in terms of simple geometric forms: "circles, rectangles, squares, triangles, cubes, cones, pyramids, rectangular prisms, hemispheres and hemi-cylinders." The statement on p. 74, "Regularity of geometrical form in the enclosure of space is fundamental to architecture," appears to miss the point of the Baroque.

How does one go about looking at architecture? P. 74: "As spatial enclosure is the main concern of architecture, the first way to look at a building, whether one is inside it or outside, is to see what manner of enclosure it makes—to get the feeling of it not as a grouping of masses, like a mountain or a monument (still less merely as a flat pattern on one façade; buildings with an elaborate façade, but mean back and sides, do not so much offend because of the attempted deception, but more because the concentration of interest in one elevation is a denial of the three-dimensional basis of architecture), but as a combination of hollow shells of various contours." To which we can only add that if a building is looked at from the outside, it is to be studied not for the interior spaces which it encloses, but principally for the exterior spaces, the urbanistic hollows it defines.

Three clear but unoriginal paragraphs on scale, proportion and the module follow, along with a reference to the modern movement and a sub-chapter teaching the layman how to "read" a plan. The illustrations, all contemporary in theme, are effectively annotated and contribute to make this book—intended as a manual for those who want to build a house and not as a theoretical treatise on architecture—very useful and completely successful.

WALKER, ALLEN S., *The Romance of Building*, London, George Philip & Son, 1921.

In substance this is an elementary history of English architecture worked out in the light of a positivist interpretation based on the geographic and geological conditions of the places where monuments are situated. The "romance" of architecture consists in telling the story of life in former times. However, juxtaposed with others of such a different order, this provocative theme loses its significance. The attitude of the author is wholly Ruskinian and, in fact, the book's closing chapter is an apology and plea for Gothic Revival.

WILLIAMS-ELLIS, CLOUGH, *The Adventure of Building*, London, The Architectural Press, 1946.

A short book dedicated to "intelligent young citizens and their backward elders," it is written in a style brimming with British humor and accompanied by delightful sketches.

To understand a building, it must be made to speak, to answer these specific questions: 1) Are you practical? 2) Are you solidly built? 3) If you are new, how will you look in ten years, shabby or still in good condition? 4) Are you beautiful, at least to me, or if not, did you seem beautiful to those who built you, and why? 5) Do you convey some idea: are you restful or vigorous, reclining (horizontal) or erect (vertical), quiet or gay, delicate or strong, light or dark, feminine or masculine—like a birch or an oak; in short, have you a character, and if so, what kind? 6) Are you a good neighbor—do you love the Tudor barroom next door, or the Regency drugstore opposite, and the trees nearby and the church, as yourself; do you do unto them as you would have them do unto you; do the other buildings, the hills, and the trees, and in general everything around you gain or lose by your presence?

This suggests the tone of the book: a conversation on the varying of architectural fashions, the effect of politics on building and town-planning activity, the different periods in the history of architecture (the weakest part of the book), the public's preference in dwellings, the need to teach the client how to formulate clearly the building program he wants to have carried out. The last chapter is titled "On the Job" and consists of a typical discussion between architect, supervisor, builder and client.

Thus there is no theory here, but a series of practical, highly effective observations for the orientation of public taste. A firm position is taken in favor of modern architecture, without apodictic cultural affirmations. In short, the spirit of the book is British modernity—a traditional benevolence, which characterizes British thought, toward idiosyncrasy.

WILLIAMS-ELLIS, CLOUGH and AMABEL, *The Pleasures of Architecture,*
Boston, Houghton Mifflin Co., 1924.
A profound admiration for Geoffrey Scott protects these authors from sharing the flat, vacuous fate of so many others (p. 68): "A spectator will often find added pleasure in a building if he remembers that voids are as eloquent as solids. The space between the columns is as purposeful and was as carefully considered by the architect as were the columns themselves. Indeed, on the whole, an architect has to give more thought to what is not than to what is built . . . A building is an act of enclosure whereby a parcel of space is set aside for some purpose."

The book consists of: 1) an excellent account of architectural thinking from the Victorian period on; 2) a discussion of the relative value of the theories by which a building must express its construction, its purpose, or the architect's mind; 3) criticism of the physio-psychological and geometric-mechanical theories of architecture, whose objective veracity the authors question; 4) the observation that the public takes very little interest in the personal life of architects, particularly of Englishmen from Inigo Jones on; 5) a search for psychological traits common to all who practice architecture; finally, 6) an essay on the practice itself, another on architectural education, and long chapters on the characteristics of private and public buildings.

Written without knowledge of modern functionalist architecture, the book is, nevertheless, full of acute observations and makes useful reading. About the true and proper "pleasure of architecture" it tells very little.

YOUTZ, PHILIP N., *Sounding Stones of Architecture,* New York, W. W.
Norton & Co., 1929.
By comparison with the inhibited empiricism of half-truths of

many English writers, American pragmatism has all the advantages of openmindedness, of a plethora of vivid suggestion, despite its confusions and almost total absence of system. The following quotation will suffice to show the absolute ignorance of spatial concept (p. 32): "As fine art, architecture is an original composition of masses, planes and lines into a three-dimensional pattern in space. The artist or architect works out his design in terms of form, symmetry, proportion and shadow . . . Architecture . . . is a kind of sculpture unhampered by the meager vocabulary of the forms of man and beast; not a sculpture of restless roving bodies, but one of repose, of strong materials in equilibrium, of statics. Here is a sculpture where heroic size is the rule and where imposing perspectives give the art an epic setting."

The value of this book, however, consists in its attempt to illustrate all aspects of architecture, not only the esthetic. The titles of the chapters indicate the range of the subjects treated: 1) *Visual History*, in which architecture is interpreted as a document of political-economic civilization; 2) *Tools of Stone*, in which a building is analyzed functionally as one of man's means for multiplying his power of control over the world around him; 3) *Solid Geometry*, in which architecture is judged with respect to that mathematical science of its realization; 4) *Still Passion*, in which the life and sensuality of materials are described, while criticism is directed at the architects who consider them mute and utilize them mechanically, without awareness of their organic qualities and their response to light; 5) *Language Without Words*, in which the author defends the practical usefulness, not the value, of studying styles; 6) *Pure Art*, which concerns design or formal values; 7) *Experimental Variety*, which discusses the empirical thinking governing construction, as distinct from the scientific progress analyzed in the third chapter.

The value of the separate discussions is relative; the worth of the book lies in its theoretical framework (p. 175): "The practice of dissecting architecture into its parts and distilling design into an immaterial substance of only logical content may be defended only for purposes of study and investigation. The method of analysis always incurs the danger that we may not be able to get the parts together again. Spacial [*sic*] forms may become the disembodied soul of architecture doomed to a restless wandering existence. All life vanishes from the organism

270

dissected into its delicately adjusted parts . . ." This awareness is what makes the chapters interesting in themselves and not mere categories of predetermined ideas.

Among other books in similar vein, see:

BLOMFIELD, REGINALD, *The Mistress Art*, London, E. Arnold, 1908; *The Touchstone of Architecture*, Oxford, Clarendon Press, 1925.
CAFFIN, CHARLES H., *How to Study Architecture*, New York, Dodd Mead, 1917.
WALLIS, FRANK E., *How to Know Architecture*, New York, Harper & Bros., 1910.

It should not be necessary to repeat how much the author of this book owes to the writings of contemporary architects (in particular to Frank Lloyd Wright, Le Corbusier and Mendelsohn) once it has been stated that his aim has been to seek a modern critical perspective. For a bibliography of their writings, see the author's *Storia dell'Architettura Moderna*.

NOTES

1. *Is the Modern Spirit Anti-Architectural by Nature?* Vitale (*L'Estetica dell'Architettura*, Bari, 1928, pp. 5-20) discerns one of the reasons for today's lack of interest in architecture in the esthetic postulates of Croce and Bergson. These postulates, according to Vitale, have favored a sensitivity toward artistic forms which can be developed in *time*, in a spiritual attitude negating the material and which presumably can find adequate expression only in music.

"To construct in space," Vitale writes, "is the aim and end of architecture; but space is anti-spirit; it is pure extension, absolute and complete realization, while spirit is pure and continuous tension, the everlasting condition of becoming. Thus, for modern thought, architecture really seems something too closely tied to the material and is quasi-extraneous and hostile to spirit. It is an inferior form of art that can acquire dignity only through its spiritualization with the lapse of time (as in ruins, archeological remains and ancient monuments), when it becomes a document of human life inserted into the course of history."

The author estimates, in short, that modern lack of interest in architecture is due to the persistence of a romantic mentality which, annulling space and material, bases itself on the psychologically fragmented, on an inability to synthesize and realize, a current taste for all that is fleeting, incomplete and in the process of formation; and so to an antagonism to all that which can be completely realized, such as a building. According to Vitale, in contrast to the movement of a drama or symphony, it is the static, immobile character of architecture—which does not lend itself to continual renovation, interpretation in time or realization according to the state of mind of the moment—that keeps it from appealing to modern sensibilities. Vitale quotes Foscolo's definition of architecture: "Most unfortunate of the arts, precisely because it is confined and constrained to remain exactly what it is."

We shall have occasion to show in the context of this study—not through philosophic or scientific demonstration, but in the more direct experience of architectural analysis—how this concept of architecture as an a-temporal art has now been superseded. It would be well to caution the reader that, from now on, whenever we speak of space in architecture, we refer to the idea of *space-time*, which has been accepted by modern science and which, as we shall see, has a specific application in the criticism of architecture. It is only for brevity that we use the word *space* instead of *space-time* and it will appear evident in our argument that the static quality and lack of tension attributed to architecture by traditional esthetics are not acceptable in the spatial conception we are presenting.

2. *Love, Sentiment and Architecture.* In Chapter V, in a section dealing with the physio-psychological interpretation of architecture, we shall discuss the inaccuracy of the thesis that architecture does not express feelings, states of mind or tragedy.

Vitale is among those who insist on such a thesis: "Architecture appears to us as an absolutely anti-tragic art or, better still, as an art in which the tragic element must, of necessity, find its equilibrium . . . If there is a conflict in architecture, it takes place exclusively between the spirit of construction and mute, hostile material; but the latter inevitably ends by being completely tamed by the yoke of form, and the victory always goes to the spirit. This character of architecture differentiates it substantially from all the other arts which we may call *expressive*, in that they express feelings or concrete ideas; architecture, on the contrary, succeeds in arousing particular feelings or states of mind by expressing only abstract ideas or, better expressed, simply by realizing these abstract ideas in material terms." (*Op. cit.*, pp. 41-42.) We shall see how modern criticism has destroyed this bleak view of architecture and, by sharpening its sensitivity, has grown capable of "reading" the rich variety of expression in building.

Vitale goes on to say: "The absence of an emotional content in architecture is one of the most salient features of its esthetic, since it is due precisely to this absence that the gamut, so to speak, of the architecturally beautiful is so limited, excluding as it does many values of emotional nature. However, to the same absence is also due that sense of calm tranquility, of elevation, of solemnity and of liberation which architecture succeeds in giving us and by which it attains a true symbolic representation of a transcendent world, free of passions and gov-

274

erned by unbreakable laws, a world in which order does not suffer and does not admit deviations, and in which absolute ideas of peace, equilibrium and justice seem to be achieved in stone for eternity."

But what freedom from passion is there in Michelangelo's architecture? What unbreakable laws in the Baroque period? What harmonies, equilibriums, justices and eternities in any of the thousands of today's tenements on the fringes of our cities, in which millions of families suffocate? An ultimate harmony and equilibrium may be manifested in fine architecture, but they are also manifested in a fine symphony, novel, drama or tragic poem; in other words, they are attributes of art, not of a particular artistic activity. In truth, not only is it possible to have a psychological history of architecture, as we shall see in Chapter V, but such an interpretation has been continually arising in architectural criticism, and there is no reason why it should not. Architecture arouses an infinity of reactions and whoever learns to see its interior spaces soon realizes that they are profoundly dynamic and dramatic. A transcendental, inhuman, lifeless vision of architecture is exactly antithetical to our own organic point of view, a view which must be made general, if this art which encloses and thus intimately affects human activity—precisely because it strikes the most secret and intangible self, the unconscious—is to excite an interest in those who spend so much of their lives within it.

3. *The Difficulty of Seeing Architecture.* If the average man's attention flags, and he becomes fatigued, after an hour or so in museums, where paintings are arranged chronologically by school, imagine how it would be if he were to find paintings hung pellmell, with a Masaccio next to a Braque, followed by a Brueghel, a Renoir and then a Cosmé Tura. This is analogous to what he finds on an architectural tour of a city. If the guide books are no aid to his seeing architecture, they might at least show him how to see town planning. But they do not. In fact, knowing how to see a city is even less part of the equipment of the average man than knowing how to see its architecture.

4. *Modern Architecture and the History of Architecture.* As will be shown more clearly later, we are partisans of a modern, unbiased approach to the history of architecture and its historicization, that is, bringing its cultural and artistic tradition up to date in the light of modern architectural thought. Most architects, however, do not approach

historical monuments in the modern spirit of serious investigation. Their anti-academicism, in deeds if not in words, has too often led to a revolt against culture, which is actually a revolt against history.

If the struggle against decoration has led of necessity to a lack of interest in the decorative values of traditional architecture, it does not follow that the volumetric values championed by Functionalism and the spatial values championed by the Organic Movement have no relation to similar values in traditional architecture. Once modern awareness has established itself in architecture, it is logical to discover the modern in the old. The academician says, "Study the old to create the new" or "The new is in the old." We say exactly the contrary: "Give modern architecture depth and breadth, define its values so that the same values may at last be recognized, and thus admired, in historical architecture as well."

Three important cultural factors stand out in the last century and a half: (1) architectural historiography, (2) eclecticism in the arts, and (3) the modern movement. The first, profiting from archeological field work and the scientific methods of philological research, revealed the great ages of the past to the present. The second resulted in art's abandoning itself to imitation of the past, as the past was progressively rediscovered by historiography. The third factor, particularly modern architecture, seemed to detach itself, to split itself off from cultural tradition, to be a phenomenon outside of history, based essentially on pragmatic and functionalist ideals.

There was, of course, a direct relationship between the first and second factors. In its enthusiasm for the "cultural," art fell into erudition and there was a succession—an overlapping—of revivals: Neo-Classic, Neo-Roman, Neo-Medieval, Neo-Renaissance, Neo-Baroque. As for the third factor, the author has written a small book to help dispel the misconception that modern architecture is disconnected from history. His *Architettura e Storiografia*, Milan, Politecnica Tamburini, 1951 (as yet not available in English), was intended precisely to trace the connecting lines between cultural history and modern architecture at each phase of the latter's development.

5. *The Unity of Art and the Diversity of the Arts.* Esthetics may determine that all Art is one and that consequently every art, as a value, is identified with every other. The point we are sustaining, how-

276

ever, is not philosophical, but rather critical. It is a question of discerning where it is, in each artistic activity, that an art is best expressed; in other words, where the best point of critical application is to be found. From theories of content to the visual symbols of Fiedler and Wölfflin, the history of art criticism has been the history of the identification of more such suitable points of critical application. But architecture, as we shall see in Chapter V, has been almost excluded from this progress of criticism, which has been centered on painting and literature. Furthermore, it is now widely recognized that the analytical moment of each art, or the moment that is the object of history, is different for the various arts and specific only to each of them.

For the problem of the unity and diversity of the figurative arts, see the author's *La Storia dell'Architettura Moderna*, Milan, 1950 (in process of translation as "The History of Modern Architecture"), pp. 546-550, in which correspondences among architecture, sculpture and painting in the last century are pointed out.

6. *Space in Painting, Sculpture and Architecture.* The spatial essence of architecture has been divined by many writers, though they have not subsequently elaborated a spatial interpretation of architecture. Those who have dealt with the problem include: the ancients, like Lao Tse, who affirmed that the reality of a building does not consist in four walls and a roof, but in the space enclosed—the living space; the treatise writers of the Renaissance, who hint at the problem; Riegl, Frobenius and Spengler, in studies on "the feeling of space" (to the extent that it applies to architecture); and contemporary architects, particularly Frank Lloyd Wright and Mendelsohn. Among the writers who have understood the problem, Geoffrey Scott, who is quoted in Chapter V, stands out.

Often a brilliant intuition of space is followed by entirely extraneous considerations that serve but to generate confusion. This, as we shall see, is the case of Focillon, as of Vitale. At first, Vitale poses the problem clearly: "Painting and sculpture indubitably live in space, and in this also they may be considered closer to architecture than to poetry and music. But it is a question of a conventional, artificial space that adumbrates but does not entirely embrace reality. Painting has in fact a two-dimensional space—the plane; and three-dimensional reality is simulated by technical effort, by the play of shadows and the knowledgeable use of perspective. Sculpture, it is true, lives in three-dimensional space, like architecture, but in the last analysis this space is only superficial in character and can readily be reduced to a plane. In a certain sense we may say that sculpture revolves around reality, but can never embrace it entirely. . . . A statue is fundamentally a multiple surface, a polyhedron; true it lives in space, but this space remains external to it, is not contained in it. . . . In architecture, however, the space is not only external, but also and principally internal; it is not used in one of its relationships, as a simple surface, but in the complex of its constructive relations, as volume and mass. We may say, in a certain sense, that in architecture, space, though maintaining its essential character of pure extension, that is, void, somehow succeeds in achieving a corporeal appearance and in solidifying itself. The architectural work, in short, is not only something that lives in space, but also that makes space live in it." (Vitale, *op. cit.*, pp. 28-31)

This is very clearly put. The same author, however, goes completely astray in the midst of his discourse by writing: "When a statue achieves a unitary and organic character (for example, Verrocchio's *Colleoni* in Venice or the *Laocoön* group), we are no longer before a simple piece of sculpture, but before a monument, which is equivalent to saying an architectural work." With this the difference between space in sculpture and architecture is stated as being one of size, of a quantitatively dimensional order, and so Vitale ends by negating everything that he had established earlier. This confusion between large-scaled, monumental sculpture and architecture persists throughout Vitale's book. For instance, concerning the arch used by the Romans, he writes on page 61: "Once more we can see confirmation of the observation made above, how elements in architecture influence each other reciprocally, since the resolution of the problem of weight, obtained by means of the arch, in its turn determines a substantial change in the definition of the problem of space. The arch, in fact, by making possible the construction of the bridge and the aqueduct, determines, as it were, the emergence of a new form of architecture, in which there is no longer a distinction between interior and exterior space, since there is neither space to enclose nor a room to cover. The aim of these new constructions is not that of separating, but that of uniting; and they thus reveal the first affirmation in architecture of a new concept

278

of space as continuous." But all sculpture lives in terms of this continuous space, in terms of a *lack* of interior space. The truth is that Vitale cannot bring himself to state that an aqueduct or a bridge is a sculptural object, as if this quality were pejorative. For this reason he is led into syllogisms that must obviously confuse the reader. Yet it is clear that, without being architecture itself in the spatial sense of the word, a construction lacking internal space (bridge, aqueduct, equestrian statue, monumental fountain, etc.) is still a formative element of external space, that of town planning.

7. Transcendental Space and Organic Space. It should be stated that throughout this book we refer to space in the concrete and elementary sense of the word. Our conception of space has nothing to do with the more general, almost philosophical, conception according to which space is the characteristic element of all the figurative arts.

Vitale (*op. cit.*, p. 44), after expounding the principles of Platonic philosophy, seeks to apply them to architecture in the following way: "Ideas are accordingly contained, so to speak, in a higher sphere than the intellectual sphere itself, and can be known only through concepts which are, to be precise, their representation in the intellectual field and are in the same relation to them as *becoming* is with respect to *being*. . . . It is thus clear that the history of architecture is intimately tied to concepts that control the development of architectural forms and are the refraction, in the intellectual field, of ideas destined to be actuated in a work of art. So far as architecture is concerned, these are the same geometric ideas existing in pure extension, in that abstract and, as it were, potential space which is, according to St. Augustine's maxim, contained in God. In the field of architectural esthetics, the passage from idea to concept thus marks the passage from pure extension to concrete space, since the function of architecture is precisely the determination of space as universal container, that is, the fixing of those general relations which it, as container, has with its content, the material, from which the spatial figures are produced. It is this very passage from an absolutely free and indeterminate imaginary space to an empirical concrete space conditioned by the material that marks the creation of the work of art, the effort and the torment of the creator to fix first in conceptual terms, then in tangible relations, the indistinct lines of the idea that has flashed into his mind." This obscurely colored and antiquated reasoning, by which every architectural space becomes the symbol of a space-idea, will be illustrated further in Chapter V in our discussion of philosophic and scientific interpretations of architecture. It is clear, however, that even if this reasoning were applicable to Classic, still better to Neo-Classic, building, for example to Renaissance buildings with a plan around a single center, it has no such application to Christian, Gothic, Baroque and modern space, which does not derive from Platonic concepts of spatial figures, but has an exact relation to man, being immanent in nature. It is obvious that a purely geometrico-conceptual view of space consequently produces the confusion over the non-expressiveness of architecture, mentioned above in Note 2.

Modern criticism, having abandoned transcendental misconceptions of space on the one hand and, on the other, the biological deductions of the theory of *Einfuehlung*, is now in a position to study organic space—space as created by man to correspond to all his material, spiritual and psychological requirements, integrally considered. This is the space which everyone sees and in which everyone lives, the knowledge and experience of which must be evoked not philosophically or conceptually, but directly and concretely.

Implicit in the transcendental conception of space is a critical position that repeats the dubious conception of "progress in art." Vitale (*op. cit.*, p. 48) says, in fact: "Since architectural form—as opposed to geometric form, which is pure abstraction—is always something concrete and material, space conceived exclusively in its terms and, in a certain sense, almost generated by it, also acquires a material character. This materialistic conception is, moreover, chronologically the earliest, in short, the most gross, in all fields of human thought; and in this respect the development of architecture may be synthesized as the progressive passage from a primitive and material conception of space, considered as limited and in the guise of discrete quantity, to a more spiritual and evolved conception, in which space is thought of as simple extension, as an infinite continuum, as pure quality." In this study the word *space* is used, in Vitale's words, in its "material and gross" sense, as architectural space and not as space-idea. We shall see that exterior or urbanistic space is not infinite and that the progress, mentioned by Vitale, from closed to continuous or infinite space follows anything but a straight line in the history of architecture. (It will suffice here simply to offer in evidence the spatial concept of *cinquecento* architecture in contradistinction to that of Gothic. This will be discussed in more detail in Chapter IV.)

To establish the concrete, tridimensional or architectural meaning of space, distinguishing it from that representable in a painting, does not mean identifying architectural with physical space. A confusion of this kind would be absurd, since all of architecture abounds with examples of spaces vast and infinite, though dimensionally small, and of spaces mean and confined, even though physically colossal. (On this misunderstanding of space as interpreted in the physical sense, see *Storia dell'Architettura Moderna*, pp. 355-357, 362-363.)

8. *Possibilities for a History of Architecture.* Studies in the history of architecture, extended and intensified in Italy during the last twenty years, but carried out predominantly under the influence of a positivist mentality, have generated a critical inhibition, a depreciation of ideas in favor of data, if not of dates. The historian Giovannoni, for example, has repeatedly remarked that ours is not a moment of historical synthesis, but rather one of research and of checking data, of preparing and coordinating technical studies on building organisms, of accumulating raw, scholarly material. If this opinion seems to have been justified insofar as it has spurred serious research based on the most verifiable and valid methods, it has also created the current critical point of view that thinking must be called to a halt, that history must stop and wait (who knows how long) until all possible analytical material has been first accumulated. And so the historian of architecture has found himself, with respect to the archeologist and his data, in a position similar to that of the architect with respect to the building industry. The architect cannot do without the building industry and often a development in structural science and technique may suggest new architectural forms and possibilities. The building industry in itself, however, cannot create architecture. Analogously, archeological and philological production, with its discoveries and documents, may often sweep away a critical interpretation and provide elements for a newer one; but it can never in itself become the producer of critical works. For this reason, it certainly seems questionable to set as a prior condition for historical synthesis, the completion of philological research. (On this, see the author's *Lo stato degli studi e l'insegnamento*

281

di storia dell'architettura ["The present state of research and university teaching in architectural history"], a report to the Fifth National Congress of the History of Architecture, Perugia, September 1948. (See also reports of the First International Assembly for the Figurative Arts, Florence, published in the Proceedings, *Edizioni U*, Florence, 1948, pp. 61, 211, 236.)

9. *Urbanistic Function of Façades Independent of Interior Space.* In many examples of the Baroque, the independence of the exterior walls was not at all arbitrary, but corresponded to a then new concept of urban spaces. The Baroque aimed at a continuous "narration," an uninterrupted definition of street or square; it rejected the isolated volumetrics of the Renaissance. The walls of a building, and especially its façades, no longer constitute the limit of the interior space of the building, but of the interior space of the street or square, and are thus to be characterized in terms of the urbanistic void they help create. (In this connection, see *Architettura e Storiografia*, pp. 76-86, which contains analyses of the principal Baroque piazzas of Rome.)

10. *Architecture and Cubist Research.* A more exhaustive description of the abstract, non-objective movements following Cubism, and of their influence on modern architecture, may be found in the *Storia dell'Architettura Moderna*, pp. 25-42, 546-550. The work of modern masters shows how they have surpassed the limited programs of the schools of painting and plastic art in which they liked to class themselves. Le Corbusier transcends Ozenfant's Purism; as do Gropius, Mies and Oud the Neo-Plasticism of Theo Van Doesburg; Mendelsohn and Gaudi, Expressionism. When an abstract, non-objective movement fails to find an architect who can go beyond its pictorial and plastic limits, it fails to produce an architecture. Such was the case of Italian Futurism.

11. *Identity Between Town Planning and Architecture.* The spaces that we here descriptively call *exterior* and that are exterior with respect to a building, but interior with respect to the city, are to be interpreted by the same method we have adopted for interior spaces. (See *Storia dell'Architettura Moderna*, pp. 550-551, which shows how every architectural conception has an equivalent urbanistic one. This is true for every period in architectural history and, accordingly, an identical methodology may be established for historical studies in town

282

planning as in architecture. See *Metodologia nella Storia dell'Urbanistica* ["Methodology in the History of Town Planning"], a general report by the author at the Eighth National Congress of the History of Architecture, Palermo, September 1950.)

12. *Motion Picture Representation of Architecture.* The function and limits of motion pictures in illustrating architecture are the subject of an article, *Architettura per il cinema e cinema per l'architettura* ("Architecture for Cinema and Cinema for Architecture"), by the author, published in the review *Bianco e Nero,* Rome, Vol. XI, nos. 8-9, Aug.–Sept. 1950.

13. *Greek Town Planning.* The architectural conception of pure volumes, free of internal spatial rhythms, has its correspondence in a town planning that does not enclose its voids, but opens, "unfocuses" them to infinity. Like the theater, Greek town planning of the Classic age has the horizon for a backdrop. This conception was thrown into crisis by the city consciousness of the Hellenistic world: at Pergamo the buildings were set together so as to form a unified picture; the theaters erected great stage settings that cut off the horizon. (See the author's *Lo spazio interno delle città ellenica* ("Internal space of the Hellenic City") in the review, *Urbanistica,* Vol. XIX, no. 3. Jan.-March 1950.)

14. *Greece and Christianity.* At Syracuse (pl. 5), having screened the exterior intercolumniations and opened up the walls of the *cella* with arches, the Christians created a fabulous masterpiece out of the Temple of Athena—a spatial rhythm conditioned by and within Greek proportions.

15. *Originality of Ancient Rome.* Franz Wickhoff revealed, in his *Die Wiener Genesis,* the original character of Roman painting and sculpture, and identified the spatial features in their creation of illusion and in their method of continuous narration. Roman architecture has unfortunately not had so perceptive an interpreter as Wickhoff, but through the fundamental, philosophical unity of the arts, his findings might well be applied to architecture. The continuous narration of the Imperial forums, the static urban spaces, all closed off by structures, the Pompeiian house segregated from the outer world and turned inward on its courtyard, the great stage-sets that close the horizons of the Greek theater, the amphitheater that is a doubling of the theater on itself—are all elements of the same illusionistic intention and of that

continuous narrative style by which architecture is urbanistically resolved. (See the author's *A quarant'anni dalla morte di Franz Wickhoff* ("Forty years since the death of Franz Wickhoff"), inaugural lecture of academic year 1949-1950, in *Annuario*, Istituto Universitario di Architettura di Venezia, Venice, 1950.)

16. *San Miniato al Monte.* The formal link between S. Maria in Cosmedin and S. Ambrogio, Milan, is provided by S. Miniato, Florence (pl. 9, fig. 19). Here the artist does not limit himself to dividing the colonnaded rhythms of the longitudinal walls, but, with transverse partitions, proves his intention of achieving a three-dimensional quality, though it is expressed by a figurative vocabulary of simple planes.

17. *The Free or Open Plan in Modern Architecture.* At the center of the German Bauhaus movement, Walter Gropius has interpreted the principle of the free or open plan differently from Le Corbusier and Mies (pls. 15, 20). Composing with volumes that were block-like, but freely articulated on the terrain, he thus freed windows from the constraint of a fixed proportional relationship to the façades. (Every modern architect applies the principle of the open plan in a different way. Regarding this, see *Storia dell'Architettura Moderna*, pp. 537-539, 541-543.)

18. *"Growth" in Building.* The elastic and expansive quality of English Gothic, of medieval town planning and of the modern Organic Movement may give rise to confusion in the reader's mind. He may imagine that a building can thus expand endlessly, which is contrary to the very definition of a work of art as complete, unchangeable, inevitable and satisfying in every aspect. This would be a confusion of the genetic process of creation with its final expression in a work of art. The *process* may be elastic, expansive, narrative; the *result* must be definitive and unchangeable. (See *Storia dell'Architettura Moderna*, pp. 368-371.)

INDEX OF NAMES

Pages on which illustrations appear are indicated by numbers in italic.

INDEX OF PLACES AND STRUCTURES

Pages on which illustrations appear are indicated by numbers in italic.